# MAN
# WAS NOT BORN
# TO CRY

# Writings by Joel S. Goldsmith

| | |
|---|---|
| *A Message for the Ages* | *Rising in Consciousness* |
| *A Parenthesis in Eternity* | *Seek Ye First* |
| *Awakening Mystical Consciousness* | *Showing Forth the Presence of God* |
| *Beyond Words and Thoughts* | *Spiritual Discernment* |
| *Collected Essays* | *Spiritual Interpretation of Scripture* |
| *Conscious Union with God* | *Spiritual Power of Truth* |
| *Consciousness in Transition* | *The Altitude of Prayer* |
| *Consciousness Is What I Am* | *The Art of Meditation* |
| *Consciousness Transformed* | *The Art of Spiritual Healing* |
| *Consciousness Unfolding* | *The Art of Spiritual Living* |
| *God Formed Us for His Glory* | *The Christmas Letters* |
| *God, the Substance of All Form* | *The Contemplative Life* |
| *I Stand on Holy Ground* | *The Early Years* |
| *Invisible Supply* | *The Easter Letters* |
| *Leave Your Nets* | *The Foundation of Mysticism* |
| *Living Between Two Worlds* | *The Gift of Love* |
| *Living by Grace* | *The Heart of Mysticism: Vols. I–VI* |
| *Living by the Word* | *The Infinite Way* |
| *Living Now* | *The Joel Goldsmith Reader* |
| *Living the Illumined Life* | *The Journey Back to the Father's House* |
| *Living the Infinite Way* | *The Master Speaks* |
| *Man Was Not Born to Cry* | *The Mystical I* |
| *Our Spiritual Resources* | *The Only Freedom* |
| *Practicing the Presence* | *The Thunder of Silence* |
| *Realization of Oneness* | *The World Is New* |

All titles listed above can be found at www.AcropolisBooks.com.

# MAN
# WAS NOT BORN
# TO CRY

Joel S. Goldsmith

Edited by
Lorraine Sinkler

Acropolis Books, Publisher
Longboat Key, Florida

MAN WAS NOT BORN TO CRY
First Acropolis Books Edition 1998
Second Printing, 2004
Copyright © 1964, 1992 by Joel S. Goldsmith

All Bible quotations are taken from The King James Version

Published by Acropolis Books.
All rights reserved.

For information contact:
Acropolis Books, Inc.
Longboat Key, Florida
http://www.acropolisbooks.com


Book design by Palomar Print Design

Library of Congress Cataloging-in-Publication Data

Goldsmith, Joel S.,     1892–1964.
    Man was not born to cry / Joel S. Goldsmith; edited by Lorraine Sinkler.
        p.  cm.
    Originally published: Secaucus, NJ : Carol Pub. Group/Citadel Press, 1992.
    Includes bibliographical references.
    ISBN 978-1-889051-32-1
    1. Spiritual Life.     I. Sinkler, Lorraine.     II. Title

BP610.G64159 1998
299'.93–dc21
                                                            98-7112
                                                            CIP

Except the Lord build the house,
they labour in vain that build it.

Psalm 127

"Illumination dissolves all material ties and binds
men together with the golden chains of spiritual
understanding; it acknowledges only the leadership
of the Christ; it has no ritual or rule but the divine,
impersonal universal Love; no other worship than
the inner Flame that is ever lit at the shrine of Spirit.
This union is the free state of spiritual brotherhood.
The only restraint is the discipline of Soul; therefore,
we know liberty without license; we are a united
universe without physical limits; a divine service to
God without ceremony or creed. The illumined walk
without fear — by Grace."

From *The Infinite Way* by Joel S. Goldsmith

# TABLE OF CONTENTS

AWAKE ................................................... 1

CHAPTER 1 ............................................. 11

   THE SPIRITUAL NEW YEAR

CHAPTER 2 ............................................. 27

   THE ONE GREAT DEMONSTRATION

CHAPTER 3 ............................................. 41

   THE TRUTH THAT MAKES FREE

CHAPTER 4 ............................................. 57

   CHRIST RAISED FROM THE TOMB

CHAPTER 5 ............................................. 73

   WITHINNESS

CHAPTER 6 ............................................. 89

   BRINGING GRACE INTO ACTIVE EXPRESSION

CHAPTER 7 ............................................. 103

   THE POWER TO BECOME THE SON OF GOD

CHAPTER 8 ............................................. 117

   RISING ABOVE "THIS WORLD"

CHAPTER 9 ........................................... 133

    SPIRITUAL DOMINION

CHAPTER 10 ......................................... 147

    THE MEANING OF PRAYER

CHAPTER 11 ......................................... 165

    BREAKING THE BONDS OF HUMANHOOD

CHAPTER 12 ......................................... 185

    THE PRINCE OF PEACE


SCRIPTURAL REFERENCES AND NOTES ............... 203


TAPE RECORDING REFERENCES ...................... 207

# MAN
# WAS NOT BORN
# TO CRY

# Awake

WHEN YOU FIRST come to a spiritual study, it is only because some circumstance or condition of your life is in need of adjustment. You have not found the completeness of life; you have not found happiness, health, or some other aspect of fulfillment; and therefore, you are seeking the "missing link." In other words, you are always thinking along the line of an improvement in the human affairs of your existence.

During your spiritual study, you will find some degree of improvement taking place in your life, but I can assure you that you never will find all that you are seeking humanly, because it does not lie within the nature of a spiritual teaching to give you all the human good things you think you would like. In some avenues of your life, you will experience improved health, increased supply, or some other form of human happiness, but you will not find the completeness that you expected. About the time you actually realize that it never is going to happen, you will likewise perceive the reason, which is that you have been praying amiss. You have been trying to patch up or improve this human existence, and that is not the function of any spiritual message.

It is very clear from the message of every mystic that the object of the spiritual path is that we may "die" to the human experience and be "reborn" of the spirit. We learn that the spiritual kingdom—the real kingdom, the mystical kingdom—is not of "this world," not even when "this world" is healthy, wealthy, and wise.

On the mystical path, you learn that the goal of life is not the metaphysical goal of better health, a more beautiful home, a more expensive automobile, and more satisfying companionship: the goal is releasing the Soul from the tomb of human existence, more especially the tomb of the human mind.

If you have sufficient time for periods of introspection or contemplation, sit down occasionally and see to what extent you are imprisoned in your mind and in your body. Notice how little you know except what you find there, and then you will realize that all human experience is a life of imprisonment.

Every human being is in prison, the prison of the mind and the body, and during the normal human lifetime of an individual, he never gets outside of that prison. As far as most human beings are concerned, anything that is not in the mind or body does not exist, and this applies even to the most highly educated. In fact, very often the greater the education, the greater the imprisonment.

Life understood is an adventure. It is like the baby who, starting to crawl, begins to find a world outside of his crib, highchair, or playpen. Even though the child does hit his head or burn his fingers, the world he is exploring is a fascinating place. But somehow or other, by the time the child reaches adolescence he has lost all desire for searching and seeking; he has lost all desire for adventure. There is an interval of sex curiosity, but when that curiosity has been satisfied, there is nothing further to be curious about. Life is then lived in the body and in the mind.

There are some, however—explorers, artists, and adventurers—who do try to widen their horizons physically, mentally, and artistically, but only occasionally have there been one or two or three who wanted to explore the realm of the Soul.

Think of the word "Soul" for a moment and see how little you know about it, and then remember that the rest of the world knows less than you do, because you have discovered a great deal about the Soul in the writings you are reading and studying. The knowledge of the Soul, the life of the Soul, the wider horizon that the Soul encompasses is the greatest experience that can come to any individual.

The Soul is imprisoned in the tomb that we call the human experience, the tomb of the mind and body, and if we are to experience the Soul, we have to break through the limitations of the body and the mind. This, the Master called taking no thought for our life, but seeking the kingdom of God, the realm of God, the Soul. We violate this teaching by thinking of God, or the Soul, as having the function of improving our human life, when the divine instructions are to take no thought for this life or any of its aspects—body or mind or anything else—but to seek an awareness of that higher realm.

The reason that this realm of the Soul is so little known is that God is spoken of as God without the realization that God is the Soul of man. You can never find the kingdom of God until you have entered into the awareness of your own Soul, and you can see that this is an adventure because you have to leave behind the familiar aspects of life. You have to leave behind the things of the body and the mind and reach out into the humanly unknown. Not only did Admiral Byrd leave familiar waters in order to reach the regions of the North and South Poles, but he did not even know if there was a way back. Many explorers had set out for those Poles and had never returned, but they were willing to lose their human sense of life in order to venture into the heretofore unknown.

You will have absolutely no way of knowing what you are going to find when you reach the realm of your Soul, and you cannot even have a guarantee that you will get back. Those who have been that way before you have made no maps, either going or coming. We know that the way is the way of meditation and that a teacher can serve as a guide, but that teacher can carry you only so far into the practice of meditation, and then you are on your own.

Some become so frightened at the first glimpse of the Soul realm that they never go that way again. God is light, and to come face to face with that light is more blinding in its intensity than to look directly into the hot sun. So, if it has been frightening, it takes an adventurous spirit to make more than one attempt. It is not that God is frightening, but that the human senses are frightened by the unknown. Actually there is nothing to fear.

As a rule, progress on the spiritual path is so gradual that the entire way is a joy. Here and there, there will be experiences that are momentarily frightening because you had perhaps expected something different. For example, you may have thought that every day would be a joyous experience, whereas those periods are few, and the periods of barrenness and emptiness and the feeling that you are separated from God are many. Actually these are more necessary to your spiritual unfoldment than sitting on "cloud nine," because without that complete barrenness you are a vessel already full, and nothing new can enter. You have to lose your concepts of God and what you expect of God.

I wish I could use as a title for a book *Santa Claus God* because that is what the majority of the concepts of God are. Be assured that no one can enter the realm of the Soul with any such God in mind. You also have to leave behind all that you have heretofore expected of companionship in the human sense of companionship. You long to tell your companions what you are thinking and what you are doing, and you want to share your joys and your successes. That cannot be done on the mystical path because those who have not been there can have no way of being able to share them. Only rarely do you find a companion with whom you can share, and even then you discover that there are some things that must remain forever hidden.

Does this not account for the Master's loneliness during his three-year ministry? When he wanted to reveal some of the secrets of the fourth-dimensional life, he could take only three of his disciples with him. All twelve could never have been prepared to see that the men who lived five hundred years before the time of the Master were not only living then, but were standing right there with them and sharing with them their wisdom. He never told that to the twelve disciples—only to three—and I am sure there were some secrets he did not tell even the three. This is that "aloneness" that comes in this life when we find that we can share our accomplishments and attainments with only a very few.

The moment you enter the higher consciousness, your vision expands, and you can see events of the present, the past, and the future. It is like standing on an eleventh floor balcony where you can see for miles in all directions, whereas the man on the street is aware only of that which is taking place right before his eyes. From the higher realms of consciousness the past is visible, and the present, and the future—yet not as fortune telling. You can go back to the prophets in the Bible and see how they knew of what was to come, and what could have been done to prevent evil from happening. But the evils did happen. Why? Because no one can believe what he cannot comprehend—which is why you lose many companions on the spiritual path.

There is a practical reason for undertaking the spiritual adventure. With what is now known, it is possible to work behind the scenes and change the course of future events. This is known to the mystics who are now on "the other side of the veil" and, to the extent that they find men and women receptive to the spiritual urge, they are able to give the benefit of their wisdom to those now on earth and to exert an influence which helps to adjust human affairs.

Even without this the adventure is worthwhile because it frees your Soul from limitation. It frees your life from being just a round of getting up in the morning, eating three meals a day, and going to bed at night. This in itself is a prison.

Man was not created to be a slave—physically, economically, or mentally. The purpose of man is to show forth the nature of God. Man originally was intended to be the instrument through which, or as which, God lives on earth. This is the meaning of incarnation—God incarnated as, or in, individual man. The Prodigal symbolizes man's "lost way" and shows that man can find his way back to "the Father's house," to the divine consciousness, and live as the heir of God with the purple robe and the jeweled ring. Man is the great glory of God.

Man was not meant to cry, and all his tears are shed only because of a sense of limitation. Every tear you shed is proof of some form of limitation being experienced in your life. Man was not born to cry!

The more you search around in your body and in your mind, the more imprisoned you will become. Do not think for a moment that you are free of the body or the mind. Rather you must understand that, through your study, you are breaking out of the body and the mind into the realm of the Soul. When you reach that Realm, and even as you approach it, the mind and the body will be discovered to be more receptive to God-government and require less and less of human attention.

Eventually you will be released from this imprisonment by an act of grace. Something will happen to you—not if you just sit around and wait for it, but it will happen if you keep your thoughts struggling upward. "Thou will keep him in perfect peace, whose mind is stayed on thee.[1] ... In all thy ways acknowledge him, and he shall direct thy paths.[2] ... In quietness and in confidence shall be your strength."[3] With these efforts you prepare yourself for the act of grace that will eventually set you free. You can see now why angels are pictured with wings, and the reason I speak of "soaring thoughts," "mountaintop experiences," or "the lofty heights of consciousness." When the Soul is released, it flies upward, not in time or space, but in consciousness. It is no longer anchored to the ground. It is no longer entombed in body and mind: it is a soaring awareness, a soaring faculty.

When a person experiences physical death, it is mistakenly thought that his Soul leaves the body and flies upward. The reason I say this is a mistaken sense is that behind it there is the actual truth. As you "die daily" to the mental and physical sense of life, the Soul is released and flies upward. This is not the day of your physical death: it is the day you become alive because of the "death" of your false sense of Self. It is the day you are released from the tomb of body and mind, and then the Soul is free. Although this is taught symbolically, as in all mystical teaching, fundamentalists have interpreted it literally, just as they have the story of Jonah and the whale, which symbolizes man's imprisonment in human belief.

You know you have a body and you know you have a mind, but you have not come to know the *you* that has the body and the mind. This is the *you* that is the adventure of life, and the adventure of life is the awakening of this *you*. You are the Soul that lives. But first you must know the you that is that Soul, and then you must begin to explore, search, and seek until you find Me*, until you find your *Self*, the real *you*. This is the *you* that God sent forth to live God's life on earth, the *you* that was never born, the *you* that will never die, the *you* that for a moment is entombed in a "parenthesis," struggling to break out so as to live in the full sentence of life.

If you search your body from your toes to the top of your head trying to locate where you are, you will discover that you do not exist anywhere between the head and the toes. You cannot find your Self in any part of the body, and this should give you the first cue: "If I am not in this body, where am I? What am I?" Then the search for the man of God's creation begins. The great adventure has begun!

It is best to keep all your discoveries to yourself, because never believe you will ever find anyone having exactly your experiences. Then some day, when you are knowingly "outside the body" and realize, "I am I," you will be able to see that God has planted the fullness of himself in you so that nothing can be added to you and nothing can be taken from you, that you really live in your Self-completeness in God. You will then not only seek nothing outside, but you

---

* The word "Me," capitalized, refers to God.

will be free to share twelve baskets full every hour of the day without any thought that you are depleting yourself. Then you will be living a life of joy, heaven on earth, but not until you see *Me* as *I*\*\**AM*—see your Self as it is, not locked up in a body or mind, but incorporeal, spiritual, omnipresent, free.

Then you will know why it is written: "Weapons reach not the Life; Flame burns it not, waters cannot o'erwhelm,"[4] for you are *I*, made of the very nature of God—indestructible, indivisible, inseparable from God. Neither life nor death can separate you from life, God, love, fulfillment!

Joel S. Goldsmith

*Kailua, Hawaii*
June 30, 1963

---

\*\* The word "I," italicized, refers to God.

# ❖ 1 ❖

## THE SPIRITUAL NEW YEAR

IF THE BEGINNING of a new year remains only a calendar-wise beginning, it has no significance whatsoever and produces no assurance as to the kind of a year it can be for you or for me individually, or for anyone else in the world. Always at this time there are the traditional Happy New Years, but regardless of how many good wishes are given or received, they are without power to bring about happiness, peace, harmony, or prosperity in the new, or in any other, year.

Newspapers on New Year's Day are usually filled with predictions for the coming year; figures and statistics are examined in an attempt to forecast what will happen; but inasmuch as each person has an entirely different way of evaluating available statistics, each arrives at a different conclusion.

It would be interesting to read the predictions in the January 1 editions of last year's newspapers to see how very few of them have come to pass, for neither predictions nor wishes have power to bring about anything in our experience. Far from presenting a hopeless picture, however, this

AUTHOR'S NOTE: The material in Man Was Not Born to Cry first appeared in the form of letters sent to students of The Infinite Way throughout the world in the hope that they would aid in the revelation and unfoldment of the transcendental consciousness through a deeper understanding of Scripture and the practice of meditation.

really is the foundation for a very encouraging one because once it is realized that predictions and wishes have no influence upon the year, people can then begin to see what can be done within themselves that will have an effect upon the course of the New Year.

## *The Power of an Individual*

Everyone has not only tremendous influence upon his own life and upon the lives of those who are near and dear to him but, far more than this, he has the possibility of influencing the whole world. In fact, the course of history has often been altered by one person.

The 1960 election is an excellent example of the power of the individual. Just a few votes in this community or in that changed the results in a state and, comparatively speaking, less than half of one percent determined the result of the entire election. So when we are tempted to think how little power we have in shaping the history of our nation or of the world, let us remember how powerful one single vote or a dozen votes can be.

It should not be necessary to call to mind the power that a Moses had in his time, a Jesus, a John, a Buddha, or a Lao-Tze, a power affecting not only the events of their own day but the history of all time. No one knows what person or group of persons may affect the history of a single year or bring about far-reaching changes in the world.

Whatever change is to be brought about must first of all begin with the individual, and then gradually the circle is widened until his influence is felt in the experience of others. So we must begin with individual you and individual me in the realization that the New Year has no power within itself to be any different from the past one. In other words, during the forthcoming year, as in all previous years, some will become healthy and some sick, some wealthy and some impoverished. The blessings and problems of the year itself will not be distributed equally among all people, nor equally among countries or communities.

## Consciousness Is the Secret

What is the cause of these differences? The answer, as always, can be found in the one word "consciousness." In our humanhood, we are states and stages of consciousness, and whatever our outer experience is, is determined by our state of consciousness. The word "consciousness," therefore, contains within itself the entire secret of individual and collective life, the secret of harmony or discord.

In our early years, we have little or no control over what our consciousness is because our parents dominate our lives, and in a sense they set the pattern of our consciousness so that we really are the showing forth of their states of consciousness. They imbue us with their standards, attitudes, and prejudices. Furthermore, some of us are born full of hope, confidence, assurance, peace, and joy, while others come into the world full of fear, anxiety, and doubt.

Probably we have all known children who were really beautiful at birth and, during their earliest years, the very reflection of their mother's or father's consciousness. Later in life, when they are living under their own consciousness, they sometimes lose this beauty and whatever charm they had in their childhood unless their own state of consciousness evolves to as high a state as that of their parents. On the other hand, there have been ugly ducklings who have blossomed into beauties once the influence of their parents was thrown off and they could function on their own consciousness. Then, too, poverty complexes have often been foisted upon some children by their parents and their surroundings, and only when they are away from that influence are they able to flower or expand.

While as children we are not responsible, once we have come to an age where we begin to make our own decisions and to live our own lives, no longer either bound by the limitations of our parents or blessed by their bounties, we then have an individual life to live and an individual consciousness to unfold. This is where our education or lack of it, our environment, and our friends all begin to have some influence upon our consciousness, and from that time forth, we may evolve in much the same way that our friends, relatives, or schoolmates are evolving.

Few individuals at any time during their earth-span ever attain sufficient freedom to live their own lives. They usually live in the lives of their families, their friends, their community, and their surroundings, and they are unable to surmount these because they have not been taught that each person is an individual consciousness with individual God-given capacities, individual propensities, and individual characteristics, all God governed, and that anyone so endowed can throw off the influence of his surroundings and of the world about him and begin to live in that "liberty wherewith Christ hath made us free."[1]

Those of us who are led to a metaphysical or spiritual teaching are given the opportunity to "come out from among them"[2] and become separate. Our very first experience with such teachings reveals that we exist as consciousness, and that God is the original substance, essence, and law of that consciousness. Therefore, we can be the showing forth of infinity, eternality, and immortality; we can be the showing forth of God's grace rather than the showing forth of the kind of physical, mental, moral, or financial era in which we happen to have been born. The truth is that if we live by the grace of God we are independent of whatever is going on in this world. We need not feel that our good is dependent on favorable world conditions, nor that we can be deprived of our good by the negativism operating in the world. We must come out from this mass consciousness and begin to live our lives as individuals.

So it is, then, that when we come to a new year, we cannot expect it to hold new hope for us simply because it is new. Our great and only hope lies in the change of consciousness which may take place in us, a change that can make this year a better one than last, a richer, deeper, more harmonious and healthful one.

## *Recognize the Presence Within*

Granted that a change of consciousness is necessary in order to make our new year better in every way, how then do we determine what that state of consciousness is to be? Students of The Infinite Way already know that a consciousness imbued with truth manifests as the harmonious outpicturing of life, and that the outer form of our life is determined by the degree of truth embodied in our consciousness, or the amount of truth of which our consciousness is constituted.

Even though in reality God constitutes our consciousness, and we therefore already possess the full and complete perfect spiritual consciousness, this is only of demonstrable availability in proportion to our awareness of that truth. It will not be demonstrably available if our lives are lived by

performing our daily tasks with little or no conscious realization of a spiritual presence and power within us. Without
a continuous, conscious recognition of this presence, we are
subject to the mass human consciousness, and if it happens to
be a year of universal prosperity or of collective good health,
we probably will share in it. On the other hand, if it happens
to be a year of economic depression or a year of epidemics,
we will share in that, too.

The only way to avoid being a part of that mass mind,
which results in the kind of robot-like life that is lived by the
majority of human beings, is to begin and end our day, and
to continue throughout the day, praying without ceasing, by
recognizing that we ourselves are not living our own life, nor
is anyone else living it for us, but that God is living it:

*God in the midst of me is mighty. There is a divine presence
that goes before me to "make the crooked places straight."[3] There
is a spiritual presence and power within me that is the law of
resurrection unto my entire experience, unto my business and my
body, my profession and my health. There is a spiritual influence
within me, a spiritual presence that restores even the lost years
of the locust.* *

The continued recognition of the presence and power of
God within our very own being is what separates us from
the masses, and enables us to live a God-governed life, a
life lived under the law, the substance, and the activity
of God, the presence and the power of God. But only by

---

* The italicized portions of this book are spontaneous meditations that
have come to the author during periods of uplifted consciousness and are
not in any sense intended to be used as affirmations, denials, or formulas.
They have been inserted in this book from time to time to serve as
examples of the free flowing of the spirit. As the reader practices the
presence, he, too, in his exalted moments, will receive ever new and fresh
inspiration as the outpouring of the spirit.

acknowledging him in all our ways, keeping our mind stayed on him—only this separates us from the mass influence, saves us from the collective experience, and enables us to be a law unto ourselves.

### "Be Ye Therefore Perfect"

We become a law unto ourselves the moment that we consciously accept God in the midst of us and the son of God dwelling in us, thereby recognizing our relationship as children of God, and if children, heirs of God, joint-heirs to all the heavenly riches. But only by our conscious acceptance of this truth do we bring ourselves under God's law.

As human beings, we are not under the law of God, neither indeed can be. As human beings, we are under the laws of humanity—the law of karma, the law of cause and effect—and whatever laws are operating in human consciousness produce their effect upon us individually. It is because we have not attained the fullness of spiritual realization that we fail to demonstrate the fullness of spiritual harmony.

The command is: "Be ye therefore perfect, even as your Father which is in heaven is perfect."[4] Only in this way can we become separate and apart from universal laws and beliefs. But there is no way for a human being to be perfect. In fact, there is no way for a human being even to approach perfection. Only as we acknowledge the perfection of God in the midst of us and acknowledge God's government, reign, and law, only then can we be perfect with God's perfection, and then we find that in a tremendous measure we are separate and apart from those things that are governing and affecting the life of the people of this world.

This perfection is not gained in an instant. We have to begin where we are, not claiming perfection for ourselves, but "forgetting those things which are behind,"[5] and claiming at least for the moment that since "I and my Father are one,"[6] that oneness governs our life, and the allness of God is the measure of our capacity. We recognize, of course, that no one is demonstrating the fullness of God-capacity at this moment, but can we not rejoice if we are demonstrating such a measure of it as to enable us to live separate and apart from the sins, diseases, lacks, and limitations that otherwise would be upon us?

Let us not make the mistake that some have made in the metaphysical world, the mistake of becoming discouraged because we have not demonstrated complete harmony or complete freedom. Let us rejoice in every single measure of spiritual harmony that comes into our experience as a proof of what the ultimate can be, and will be, as we persist in this way. If we can just demonstrate some measure of our spiritual relationship to God, we will have made a beginning, but we will never accomplish the fullness until we have made that beginning.

Our life this year will be subject to God and God's government in proportion to our individual acceptance of the truth and our persistence in it. There is no way for spiritual law or spiritual truth to affect the life of those who do not consciously accept it and work with it. This is an individual matter. No one can do this for another person no matter how great a love and bond there is between them. Even after three years of companionship with the Master himself, Judas failed to show forth little but the consciousness of a betrayer. Peter denied Jesus, and all the disciples deserted him when he needed them most. This is a silent testimony of the extent to which the individual himself must embrace truth in order to demonstrate it.

### Individual Responsibility

Merely being a part of a spiritual teaching brings some measure of harmony to everyone in it. Furthermore, the consciousness of a teacher or practitioner also has an effect upon all those who come within his orbit, but this is only of temporary benefit except where the individual himself carries on and develops his own consciousness.

So it is that a teacher or a practitioner cannot guarantee what degree of spiritual harmony will be the lot of the student. He can only be an instrument for awakening the spiritual awareness of the student, and then it is the responsibility of the student to work with the principles until his own consciousness has evolved.

Similarly, no parents can guarantee what their child will be: they can only lay the foundation for the moral, ethical, and spiritual standards with which he is to face life. Children may be brought up in the most satisfactory kind of home and apparently be the most obedient and well-behaved children, but when they go out into the world, if they do not apply the lessons they have learned at home and carry them into action, they can very well become the profligates of their generation.

### Steps in Developing Spiritual Consciousness

The first step in spiritual unfoldment, a step which the student can take under guidance if he wishes, but which in the last analysis he has to take for himself, is the conscious recognition and acknowledgment of an inner God-government, substance, and law. Each one must make the realization of an inner presence a daily practice in his life. Constantly, there must be the reminder that this presence within is greater than any problem that he faces in daily living or any situation he meets in the outer world.

With this must come the conscious realization of the principle that finally proves to be the one that gives us our ultimate freedom from what the Master called "this world." When he said, "I have overcome the world,"[7] he meant that he had reached a place in consciousness where the world had no effect upon him, neither its material and mental laws nor its health and food laws nor its economic and governmental laws: none of these had any effect upon him. He had risen to a state of consciousness where he functioned completely through spiritual law.

This state of consciousness is attained first by the recognition of the God-presence within, but there is a step greater than this that has to be taken, and that is the recognition that spirit is the only power, the only law, and the only reality.

We are faced from early morning until late at night with the universal belief that there are material, mental, and legal powers. To attain Christ-consciousness, each one himself must eventually come to some recognition that spiritual power, spiritual law, and spiritual life alone are the real and the omnipresent, and that aside from spiritual law, life, and activity, material and mental laws have no power. This is the basic truth that sets men free from the conditions of this world: the realization of spiritual law or spiritual power as being the only reality.

Then we can begin, even in a small measure, to understand that when the Master said, "Arise, and take up thy bed"[8] or, "Stretch forth thine hand,"[9] he meant, "What power is there apart from God? What power is there other than God? Is sin a power? Is disease a power? Is money a power? Is law a power? Is anything really a power besides God's government?"

Gradually, we come to that place where we, too, can say, "Arise, and take up thy bed," because what we have heretofore acknowledged as power is not power; what we have acknowledged as limitation is not limitation, and has been acting as such only to the extent of our acceptance of two powers, good and evil. As long as we accept two powers, we are subject unto two powers. Therefore, along with that first step of conscious realization of the fact that there is an inner presence and power that governs the outer life, there must be this second realization that there is but one power, and it is spiritual. There is but one law, and it is spiritual; there is but one activity, and it is spiritual. All else is without power, without presence, continuity, cause, or effect, and without a law to sustain it.

The New Year, then, becomes what we make it by our inner life. True, we still go through all the human motions of performing what is demanded of us by life, carrying on our business or our profession, whatever it may be, but now always governed by this inner life.

These two steps, practicing the presence of God and changing our consciousness from the universal belief in two powers to the acceptance of the truth that there is but one power, will almost from the beginning bring a greater sense of peace and harmony into our experience. Ultimately, through this practice we shall learn that it is the inner contemplation and peace that has the power to change the history of the world, that without going out on a platform proselyting or crusading, without trying to revolutionize either religion, politics, or economics, this inner power brings about the uncovering of new ideas, new inventions, and new discoveries. Our inner contemplation changes the history of this world, and brings forth the hidden mysteries that still must come to light to bring peace on earth.

## Civilization Is Yet to Be Achieved

The world likes to believe that it is living in a period of civilization, but the truth is that civilization has not yet really begun on earth. Only its beginning stages are evident. If the word "civilization" has any meaning at all, it must mean brotherhood; it must be a relationship of brothers among men, and without that relationship it can hardly be called civilization: it is still only animality. Any failure to love our neighbor as ourselves is the measure of our lack of civilization; so it cannot be said that civilization has come to earth until there is loving of our neighbor as ourselves.

Civilization has to begin with an individual, and it has to be carried to the height to which Jesus lifted it in his Sermon on the Mount. What he taught was real civilization, and we will know that civilization only as we grow to the place where we live according to the Sermon on the Mount, where we leave behind all thought of revenge or of practicing the old eye-for-an-eye and tooth-for-a-tooth doctrine. Again, that is an individual experience which eventually becomes collective.

What we are becomes evident to the entire world that knows us, so that the inner stillness, peace, quiet, and love that we attain become a spiritual influence felt by all around us. The lack of it in us is also felt by everyone, and for this reason it is important that our life in the New Year be governed by an inner grace, an inner love for our neighbor, and a greater reliance on the truth that there is but one power, and it is spiritual, closer to us than breathing—within us.

We carry spiritual power wherever we go—up in the air or down into the sea or on the earth. In the hospitals which sometimes we must visit, or the prisons, or the homes or the lecture halls—wherever we are—we carry the spiritual presence and power of God by our conscious recognition and acknowledgment of it, and in no other way. Only by that recognition is the spiritual presence and influence so embodied within us that the place whereon we stand becomes holy ground.

In this way, then, do we keep our consciousness imbued with truth, and in proportion as our consciousness is imbued with truth are we made free of world conditions. Then we can say, "I have overcome the world."

## ACROSS THE DESK

There can be only one goal for the seeker: to know God aright. That is why the scriptures of the world play such an important role in the life of those on the spiritual path. Every great spiritual master has created his own scripture which has become a part of the spiritual literature of the world. Krishna, the first man of light of whom we have any knowledge, gave to the world the earliest recorded scripture which is embodied in the Hindu *Vedas* and the *Upanishads* which include the *Bhagavad Gita*. Lao-Tze's legacy to the world was the Way of Tao; Gautama the Buddha added to Hindu scriptures his Path; and Shankara, his great teaching of Advaita. Jesus the Christ gave us as our heritage The Sermon on the Mount, the way of life by grace. Paul left a message of living by Christ which has been added to the Christian Gospels. Nanak gave the rich teaching of the Sikhs of India. To all of this, we add other scriptures, those of the Moslems, the Persians, the Zen masters, and finally the new scripture of metaphysics in Mary Baker Eddy's *Science and Health*.

What is the purpose of all this scripture? The answer lies in the lives of those men and women who attained

God-awareness, and who were dedicated enough to share with others the heights they reached. Their only object was to help others attain this same God-awareness because they knew that attaining God-awareness is the greatest goal of life, and that only in this is man fulfilled.

Until the attainment of God-realization, man is but an empty shell, something cut off from God, not under the law of God; but in the attainment of the knowledge of God, man becomes the very presence of God, the *I Am*, the divine Son or offspring of God, the heir of God. God is revealed and fulfilled as man. God the Father, walks the earth as God the Son, for "I and my Father are one."[10] ... He that hath seen me hath seen the Father."[11] The attainment of this oneness, then, becomes the final step of God-attainment or God-realization.

The day is not too far distant when all the earth will be full of the knowledge of God. Every man will know God, and his kingdom will be on earth. When man has attained the realization of his true nature, he will live as the presence of God, through which and as which God lives. This is a life devoid of greed, lust, false ambition, fear, hate, and jealousy. This is a life through which love, joy, peace, and justice flow forth unto all. This is a life devoid of self in the attainment of Self—God as individual Selfhood.

There is a fellowship of God-realized people on earth today, and those who have seen The Infinite Way activity in different parts of the world have seen heaven being lived on earth. If this fellowship would ever become an organized activity, it would no longer be a spiritual body or a spiritual family because it would then be separate from mankind— selfish, limited, and dead. The spiritual life can only be lived in freedom as one with all united in God. When we separate man from man, we lose freedom, justice, and peace. The life of the Soul is in union with God and man, as each branch can live only in union with the tree and with branches. Death lies in separating and dividing one's self from the whole.

To live spiritually is to acknowledge only one Father and one Son. To know God aright is to know one's Self.

# ❧ 2 ❧

## The One Great Demonstration

Learning the importance of meditation is one of the first requisites in the development of spiritual awareness. Regardless of our intellectual capabilities or the amount of reading or listening we may do, our spiritual capacity expands only in proportion to our ability to meditate. This spiritual awareness is developed in silence, not in thinking, in listening, or in reading. More of it can be developed in one minute of silence than in twenty-four hours of reading. For this reason, reading and studying are but tools which we use to enable us to reach that inner silence known as meditation.

As we meditate and open this inner Soul or spiritual faculty, we shall not only understand things that we knew about and never before understood, but things that we may never even have heard of before. In the stillness and quiet of the silence, we are able to receive what cannot be heard through the ears. The more often we meditate—not the length of time in any one period, but the number of times in each twenty-four hours, even if each time be only one minute, or two or three—the more rapidly will our spiritual awareness be developed, and spiritual harmony brought into our experience.

When our eyes are closed and we are in the darkness within, we find the entire kingdom of God there, ready to pour itself into our mind, our body, our home, our business, and even into our purse. With eyes closed, our attitude is

27

one of receptivity as though we were inviting God to speak to us, or as though we were inviting the spirit to flow forth through us. Our part is to remember that the fullness of God is within us, and as we are still, the spirit makes itself manifest in our experience.

## Infinity Is the Measure of Our Being

The first and greatest principle of The Infinite Way, the principle upon which its entire activity has been founded, is that God constitutes individual being, your being and mine.

*God is the mind of me, the life, the Soul, the spirit, and God is my capacity. I have access to infinite intelligence, to infinite, eternal life. I have access to infinite supply, infinite harmony, peace, and perfection—to all of these because I have access to infinity.*

This infinity can be brought forth into our experience only in proportion to our knowledge of truth. "Ye shall know the truth, and the truth shall make you free."[1] It is not the truth that makes us free: it is *knowing* the truth. Therefore, we must know that nothing less than infinity constitutes the nature and character, the quality and quantity of our being.

We can demonstrate that infinity in proportion to our realization and attainment of this understanding. Merely the knowledge that God is our mind will not enable us to be infinitely intelligent. It is the conviction that God constitutes our mind which makes the infinite wisdom of God available as our individual capacity to understand, to know, to discern, and to bring forth. Jesus said, "I can of mine own self do nothing,"[2] and we can go still further and say, "I of my own self can *be* nothing. I of my own self can *have* nothing; but because of my oneness with God, all that the Father has is mine." This infinity of God becomes individually ours because of our divine relationship to God and our conscious awareness of this truth.

### *The Presence of God Is the Only Demonstration Necessary*

"Take no thought for your life, what ye shall eat, or what ye shall drink; nor yet for your body, what ye shall put on.... Your heavenly Father knoweth that ye have need of all these things."[3] This is the principle upon which our entire life's demonstration must be founded. We should never attempt to demonstrate anything at any time: not health, wealth, supply, business, home, or companionship. If we do, we are demonstrating finiteness or form, and all form is destructible and limited.

Instead of taking thought for what we shall eat or drink or how we shall be housed or companioned, we must seek first the realization of God, the consciousness of the presence of God. Then, God will appear as infinite form—as supply, companionship, home, transportation, safety, or security.

God is "the health of my countenance[4] ... The Lord is my rock, and my fortress ... He is my shield, and the horn of my salvation, my high tower, and my refuge."[5] Why then attempt to demonstrate health or safety? Our need is not the demonstration of high towers, shelters, or fortresses: our need is the demonstration of God because God is the only high tower, the only real protection, the only One capable of hiding us from trouble of every kind, whether bombs, poverty, or discord. In The Infinite Way, we do not try to demonstrate peace: we demonstrate the conscious awareness of the presence of God, and as we gain that awareness, we find our peace, rest, contentment, abundance, our allness. "Where the Spirit of the Lord is, there is liberty,"[6] liberty in the true sense of the word: freedom, justice, equality, mercy, benevolence, abundance.

The entire basis of demonstration in The Infinite Way and a major principle upon which all the work is founded is the demonstration of the consciousness of God's presence. There is no room for any other demonstration. I know of no way of reducing fevers or lumps; I know of no way of bringing about the employment of the unemployed; I know of no way of settling disagreements in families, businesses, or in communities. Nevertheless, the work of The Infinite Way has settled disputes between management and labor; it has brought harmony into families and into every kind of human relationship; and yet none of us in this work would know how to go about accomplishing these ends except in one way.

When we are called upon for help, through a contemplation of truth, what we might call treatment, we bring ourselves to a place of stillness in which the presence of God is realized and actually felt. God becomes something more than a word or a concept we hold in mind: God becomes an actuality, a reality, a presence which can be felt, realized, and cognized. It is an actual presence which makes itself tangible within us, so that we can almost believe that we have seen God face to face. I do know that if I have not seen him face to face, I have at least felt his touch many times. I have felt that gentle presence within, and sometimes without. But this is brought about by contemplation of God, by dwelling and meditating on God as an ever-present reality.

Regardless of the name or nature of the problem facing any one of us, the solution lies in the realization of this presence of God within, and then letting the presence of God go before us to prepare a place for us, walk beside us as protection, and come behind us as a rear guard. God cannot be defined or analyzed, but God can be understood as an invisible presence.

Let no one ever make the mistake of trying to understand what God is. God is beyond our comprehension because our comprehension is finite, and God is infinite. It was well said by Maimonides, the Hebrew mystic, "To say that God is, is all that can be known about God. To say that God is good, or God is powerful, or God is present, or God is love, is to say no more than that God is." That is the only acknowledgment that is really necessary. God is, and with this comes the realization, "Yes, not only God is, but God is closer than breathing, nearer than hands and feet. The place whereon I stand is holy ground." And I hear the Father say, "'Son, thou art ever with me, and all that I have is thine'[7]—yes, all that I am, thou art."

Yet of that infinite nature, of all that quantity and all that quality, we can show forth only whatever degree of realization we may attain. But to attain even a grain, even a touch, of the realization of God is to bring miracles into our experience.

### *God Appears as the Fulfillment of the Need of the Moment*

When Moses was leading the Hebrew people out of Egypt, we are told, he was guided by a cloud by day and a pillar of fire by night. But I am sure that he never thought of demonstrating such things. Surely, all that Moses ever dreamed of was the presence of God, knowing that where he went, God went with him, knowing that he could not be outside of God because he lived and moved and had his being in God, and God in him.

By Moses' dwelling in that realization, God's presence appeared as a cloud by day and as a pillar of fire by night, and when it was necessary, Moses' realization of God appeared as manna falling from the sky. Did Moses think of manna, or did he think only of God's presence? Did he not realize: "Where I am, Thou art. Where Thou art, I am, for I Am That I AM. We are one."

We are told that the Master Christ Jesus demonstrated loaves and fishes for the multitudes, but what he really did was to look up to heaven and recognize God's presence, and that recognition of God's presence appeared as loaves and fishes, for that was the need of the moment.

Elijah, too, demonstrated God's presence. When he fled into the wilderness, a raven brought him food. He found cakes baked on a stone in front of him. A poor widow shared what little she had with him. He was living in the conscious awareness of God's presence, the awareness of "Where Thou art, I am; and where I am, Thou art, for we are one," and then when the time came for food, it appeared. If it was necessary for a raven to bring it to him or for a poor widow to share her mite with him, that is how God appeared at the moment. But I am sure that Elijah never thought of ravens bringing food or of cakes being baked on stones for him.

Elijah, as revealed in Scripture, was a man who lived, moved, and had his being in the constant awareness of God, never for a moment living outside the atmosphere of God. He never took thought for what he should eat or drink or wherewithal he should be clothed. He had his God, and that was his sufficiency.

Paul had that same reliance: "My grace is sufficient for thee."[8] It does not say that money was his sufficiency or security or property. It says, "My grace is sufficient for thee." And where is God's grace? It must fill all space since nothing of God can be localized in time or space. There is no time or space where God is not and where the allness or the fullness of God is not. So with all our getting, we must get God, and then all these things will be added unto us.

"In thy presence is fulness of joy; at thy right hand there are pleasures for evermore."[9] With all of our taking thought, we should take thought only for God's presence because when we are in God's presence, we are in the presence of fullness, the fullness of health, the fullness of morals, supply, good, harmonious relationships, and the fullness of service, with twelve basketsful left over. This transcendental presence, that which we call God-consciousness, is the substance of our demonstration. When we have the substance, which is God, we have any and every form necessary to our unfoldment or demonstration.

The problem of supply is an ever-present one, since there is never a day or a moment of a day when there is not a need for supply in one form or another. One of these forms, and a very necessary one, is money, but money always takes the form necessary at a particular time and place. As we travel, I have noticed that in the United States, money appears as dollars, in England as pound notes and shillings, in Germany as marks, and in Switzerland and France as francs. Very rarely does anyone give us dollars in Europe, Asia, or Australia, and very seldom does anyone give us any currency other than dollars in the United States. And why is this? It is because supply, God, is omnipresent, but it appears as the form necessary to the immediate experience.

If the need were not money, but food, it would appear as food. If the need were transportation, it would appear as transportation. The idea is to take no thought for the *form* of supply, for the *form* of demonstration, but rather take thought for the substance. And God is the substance, whether the need is for a high tower, a fortress, or the health of our countenance. God is the necessary essence, substance, the all-in-all of demonstration; and the form takes care of itself.

### *Stages of Spiritual Awareness*

Not all men are at the state of consciousness where they can rest in complete reliance on the spirit with no concern for demonstrating the things of this world. Mankind is made up of unfolding states of consciousness, and it is only gradually that men evolve from the material to the mental level, and eventually to the spiritual level of consciousness, where the goal of life is the demonstration of the presence of God.

The various metaphysical and spiritual approaches to life that have been given to the world by men and women of dedication represent teachings suitable to different states of consciousness, but no one can truthfully say that one is right and the others are wrong.

In the material state of consciousness, where material force, power, and substance are all that are known, it is certainly not wrong to avail oneself of medication and surgery or any and all help that *materia medica* offers as an aid to health because that is the purpose of those things on the material plane.

As the material state of consciousness is replaced by the mental, however, a person may at first use far less of material remedies, far less of material forces and powers, and more and more of the mental. This does not mean that one is right and the other wrong: it simply means that these are the expressions of two different states of consciousness.

The farther a person goes in the mental realm, the less he will use the material forces of the world, and in time, even less of the mental because the higher he goes in the mental realm the more he learns to rely on intuition rather than on mental power. As the mental realm slowly gives way to the spiritual—and these, by the way, are not synonymous, but two entirely different states of consciousness—less and less of the mental will be used until, if one rises high enough, none may be used at all. The greater the spiritual awareness attained by the student, the less will he use mental powers.

It is all a matter of different states and stages of consciousness. It must be recognized that on the material plane there are always two powers, a greater and a lesser, and always the greater power is used to overcome the lesser. Much the same thing applies in the mental realm. The person of strong mentality—the person who has the greatest concentrated power of thought and the most concentrated ability to manipulate and project thought, the person who can give the most emphatic treatment—is always able to dominate the one of weak mental capacities. So again in the mental realm as in the physical realm, there are two powers with the greater overcoming the lesser.

In the spiritual realm, however, this is entirely eliminated. In the spiritual realm, *there is no power.* A great deal has been spoken and written about using spiritual power, or God-power, but there is no such power to be used, nor anyone who can use it. No one has ever been able to use God-power because in spirit there is no power.

God is. That is all that can be known. But God is not power, nor is God a power over anything, except in the sense that God is that which is the substance, the essence, the law, and the creative unfolding of all form. God is a power unto its creation only in the sense that God is the creative activity, the substance, and the law which unfolds and maintains and sustains its creation, but it is never a power *over* anything.

## *Let God Use Us*

God-power cannot be used. No one has ever been able to use it, not even Jesus Christ who said, "I can of mine own self do nothing ... The Father that dwelleth in me, he doeth the works."[10] But God reveals itself * in the stillness and in the absence of power, and where the presence of God reveals itself, there is harmony and liberty. God does not create that harmony or liberty, nor does he bring it: God is it. The presence of God is peace, health, and safety; the presence of God is food and clothing and raiment. God does not give us these things: God is these; and in the silence, God manifests itself as the very life of our being, as the very light unto our feet, as the very presence that goes before us. God's presence is made manifest as infinite harmony, infinite abundance, infinite allness.

Only in the degree that we can be still and silent can God perform its wonders through us. None of us can ever use God, but God can use us. God can live through us, in us, and as us. It is God doing it—not we. On this point lies the whole difference between success and failure in the spiritual realm. The person who tries to use spiritual power is merely

---

* In the spiritual literature of the world, the varying concepts of God are indicated by the use of such words as "Father," "Mother," "Soul," "spirit," "principle," "love," or "life." Therefore, in this book the author has used, at appropriate times, the pronouns "he" and "it," or "himself" and "itself," interchangeably in referring to God.

using the power of his own mind because no one can ever use the infinity which is God.

We can be still, be still and *let*, and if or when we can be still enough, God will function as our very being. God will appear as the intelligence of our mind, as the skill of our fingers, as the voice of our throat. It will be God using us, not our using God.

You can use your muscles; you can use your body; you can use your mind. But that is where you have to stop. You cannot use God because God is the essence of your being, and while there is a you separate from your body, there is no you separate from God. Beyond the body and beyond the mind there is a you, but that you is not separate from God. Therefore, there is no you to use God. There is only God appearing as you, God functioning and living as you. This is the meaning of incarnation. This is the meaning of the Master's saying, "The Father that dwelleth in me,"[11] and of Paul's "I live; yet not I, but Christ liveth in me."[12] The Christ is your life; God is your life; God is your being; God is the *I* of you.

### Go to God for God

There is no room in your consciousness for God *and you: God lives *as you;* God is your life; God is your mind; God is your being, and even your body is the temple of the living God. With this realization will come the understanding of oneness, immortality, eternality, and infinity, and the conviction that you are limited only in proportion to your setting yourself up as an entity separate from God. No one will ever doubt immortality once he realizes that God constitutes his being.

*I have no need of powers because the* I *that I am constitutes the all and the only power, and it is a spiritual power. There are no powers besides it. God constitutes my being and my life, and I can rest in that word.*

The Master told us, "Man shall not live by bread alone, but by every word that proceedeth out of the mouth of God."[13] As long as we demonstrate the word of God, we have an infinite supply by which to live. But we must be sure that we are demonstrating only the word of God—not its forms, but letting it appear as the form necessary.

In the last business enterprise in which I was engaged, I found my business getting worse and worse until it was necessary to ask a practitioner for help. But my business did not improve, so I had to turn to another practitioner for help, and even then it grew worse and worse. Before I had finished I had had five practitioners, and still no business. The point is that when I went to those practitioners I had only one thing in mind, and it was not God. It was more business, more orders. As far as God was concerned, I was speaking a foreign language, and God did not understand that language. But when I was removed from the business world and came into this very impractical activity of spiritual healing and teaching, the problem of lack disappeared, and the work the practitioners had done for me began to bear fruit.

Supply now came in. It came in, in accord with God's will, not mine; and in God's way, not mine; and in God's time, not mine. But it did not come as long as there was a selfhood apart from God outlining what the demonstration should be, and then trying to get God to fulfill it. Have you ever stopped to think how ludicrous that must sound? "Man, whose breath is in his nostrils"[14] going to God to get God to do something for him—and in accord with man's idea of how it should be done!

So we learn that we do not go to God for business or for dollars, nor do we go to God for health. We go to God for God, and having God we have all. We will not have all while we try to have an "I" and God. "There is no room for Me and thee," says God, "for *I* fill all space. *I* am a jealous God, and there is no room for aught but Me—Me alone, *I* am all."

### Being a Beholder

"The Father that dwelleth in me, he doeth the works.[15] ... Christ liveth in me.[16] ... Greater is he that is in you, than he that is in the world.[17] ... He performeth the thing that is appointed for me.[18] ... The Lord will perfect that which concerneth me."[19] In every one of these quotations, we are referring to a *He*, but we are identifying that He as the He within us. In that way, we are better able to understand the Master when he says, "He that seeth me seeth him that sent me.[20] ... I and my Father are one."[21]

There is no need to seek for power when this infinite invisible which is our true identity, this *He*, performs that which is given us to do. He perfects that which concerns us. All that is within us; this conviction immediately takes our gaze from out here, prevents us from believing that there is somebody in this world who can help our demonstration or somebody who can mar it. It keeps us from believing that we need pull or influence or that we need something we do not have, for we know that the one thing necessary we do have, the *He* that is within, the Father within, the Christ that liveth our life.

There is an invisible something; call it the Christ, call it God, call it the Father within, call it what you will—the spirit of God within man, the transcendental consciousness, or that transcendental presence—but realize that it is invisible, it is infinite, and it is closer to you than breathing. If you mount up to heaven, it goes there with you; if you make your bed in hell, you will find it there; if you "walk through the valley of the shadow of death,"[22] you cannot fear because it is with you. "The kingdom of God is within you."[23] You live and move and have your being in God, and God lives in you.

Had I been rehearsing the above truths, silently or orally, with eyes closed or open, I would call that a contemplative meditation. Upon finishing this meditation, I would be still and take the next step, which is, "Speak, Lord; for thy servant heareth."[24] And, because Scripture says, "He uttered his voice, the earth melted,"[25] I would keep my inner ear open, as though I really were listening for the voice of God.

Then, if I were still, an impartation would come to me from that infinite invisible: it might be a message, just a deep breath, a feeling of warmth, or it might be a feeling as though a weight had fallen away from my shoulders. But in some way, within a minute or two, I would receive an inner assurance, "it is done. God is on the field." My work for that period, then, would be complete. I would be standing consciously in the presence of God, a beholder watching God at work. Tomorrow morning the result might be apparent in my mail, on the telephone, or through a telegram; or, in some way, there might be an awareness during the day that something had taken place in my experience for which I was not humanly responsible. And I would know that the voice of God had spoken: the earth of error melted, the presence of God appeared, and peace was restored.

# THE TRUTH THAT MAKES FREE

DURING THE DAYS of the early Hebrews, the high priests and rabbis were never permitted to divulge truth to the people, so there was a long period when no one had access to truth except the few who had attained a sufficient degree of spiritualized consciousness to be able to grasp it. Moses knew the truth, but because he believed that only those who had reached a high state of consciousness were prepared to understand and demonstrate it, he permitted it to be known only by those who had attained the rank of high priest.

It was Jesus' conviction, however, that truth should be given to mankind; it should be revealed so that everyone would be free, because to know the truth does set one completely free of physical, mental, moral, and financial limitations. He, therefore, went out into Judea and taught in the synagogues, by the wayside, by the seaside, in the mountains, and in the plains—wherever two or more would gather together to hear him and he revealed the truth to them.

Jesus was crucified for telling that truth, just as throughout all generations those who have dared to tell the truth have suffered crucifixion, if not always an outward crucifixion, at least a figurative one. Men of power are afraid to let the masses know about the truth. The authorities, whether ecclesiastical or political, cannot afford to permit the world to become enlightened because when men know the truth it makes them free and they can no longer be controlled. In order, therefore, to be sure that control is maintained over the people, it is necessary to keep them in ignorance of truth.

When Christ Jesus revealed truth to his followers, evidently the truth registered with a few—only a very few, but nevertheless a few—and healing work was carried on for the next three centuries. But the principle of truth was again lost. There was dissension within the Christian movement: there was one faction headed by Paul who felt that truth should be made available to everybody, even to the Gentiles, and there were the groups headed by Peter and James who felt that only Hebrews were entitled to know the truth. After Peter's vision of the "great sheet knit at the four corners, and let down to the earth: Wherein were all manner of four footed beasts of the earth, and wild beasts, and creeping things, and fowls of the air,"1 he finally accepted Paul's thesis that truth should be preached and given to all men. So it was that internal dissension, plus the persecution from outside, began to weaken the faith and dull the awareness of those dedicated to the truth, and again it disappeared from the face of the earth.

### "To Every Man There Openeth a Way"

"But the natural man receiveth not the things of the spirit of God: for they are foolishness unto him: neither can he know them, because they are spiritually discerned."2 In his humanhood, man can never receive truth. It is not until he rises above his humanhood, until he has the spirit of God dwelling in him, that he can discern the nature of truth; and because of this, truth seems to be foolishness to him.

Therefore, in every approach to truth that has ever been revealed, the first step that is necessary is developing consciousness to the place where consciousness can receive the truth. The milk of the word is given to the babes; the meat of the word to those prepared to receive it. But heaven help us if we attempt to give meat to the babes! Those babes will crucify us—innocently, of course, but a knife in the back is just as dangerous when put there by innocence as by premeditation. Was not the crucifixion of the Master a crucifixion even though carried out by those in ignorance of the truth?

Truth itself is one, but there are many, many ways of arriving at that truth, many approaches to the truth. A person can reach truth through a religion in which there is really little of truth, but so much of devotion that it can ultimately elevate him to the truth. This is perhaps one of the least satisfactory ways of reaching it. Then, there is the way of reaching truth through the mind, using the mind as an instrument through which one ultimately attains realization. Some even attempt to attain truth through gaining control of the body, the hatha yoga practiced in India today. But, however one attempts to attain union with God, whether through physical yoga, mental yoga, yoga of service, yoga of devotion, or the greatest of all, the raja yoga of spiritual attainment, all roads lead ultimately to the truth.

Today, we have been given perhaps the most unusual opportunity that has ever been given to the world in any age, the priceless opportunity to work through the mind to the spirit, thereby going from an intellectual understanding of truth to its spiritual discernment.

The vital problem for each person is to find the approach that is most acceptable to his own state of consciousness. It is my conviction that there never will be one approach that will meet the needs of everyone because we are all different states and stages of consciousness. We all have different backgrounds, and certainly our experiences in our existence before we came to this earth-plane have been different. We cannot, therefore, all attain the heights by means of the same approach.

For this reason, then, since the religious life is such a sacred one, each person should learn to go within himself and pray for light and guidance so that he will be directed to his particular path, and when it has been revealed to him, that path should be given every opportunity to fulfill itself in him. One should not go from path to path except under divine guidance because there is that within us which can lead us home if we continue to follow our leading. If we listen to our neighbor or follow some popular approach or some approach that has performed miracles for someone else, we are not really being divinely guided. We are only divinely guided when something within us says, "This is the way, walk ye in it."[3] It says nothing about your neighbor or anyone else. All it says is, "Walk *ye* in it."

For thirteen years before my first spiritual experience, I was seeking in ignorance, not knowing how to seek. Those were years of chaos internally and externally, but always there was that inner urge assuring me, "There is a God, and God can be found." Everything else in life was chaotic, but that particular principle never wavered: "There is a God, and God can be found. Stick to it."

Then, on a specific day, it happened, and it was an experience of transformation. From the moment of that experience, I literally "died" to my entire human sense of life up to that time. Every bit of yesterday disappeared, and a whole new way of life opened up, with only an occasional memory of the days that had gone before. Eventually, I was left alone in the world without any close relatives or friends, and without a dollar. And it was then that the new life began.

This religious experience enabled me to heal, and brought about a change in my whole being and life, physically, mentally, morally, and financially. Beginning two days after that first spiritual experience, people were drawn to me for help and although they were healed, actually they were no better off than they were before except that they had attained a greater degree of material harmony. In other words, they did not understand what did it; they did not know how to make it a continuing experience, and I could not teach them because I myself did not know. And so my life became a dedication to meditation to the end that I might learn the laws underlying these healings. I had to go within to see whether what had brought forth these experiences could be revealed to me. From that day to this, my life has been a continuous series of spiritual revelations, inner unfoldments and experiences, all of which are embodied in specific principles that have been given for our study.

## *An Intellectual Knowledge of God as All Is Not Enough*

The very first and probably the most important of these working principles, and one of the most important points in the entire teaching of The Infinite Way, is the revelation regarding the origin and nature of evil, and the method of dealing with it. If I were to say to you that God is all, that God is omnipresence, that God is omnipotence, and that God is closer to you than breathing and nearer than hands and feet, I would be saying only what you and many people of the world already know. These are truths that are taught in every religion in the world, and yet wars and depressions and panics and cancer and all the other plagues of the earth continue. That countless people in the world intellectually know the truth about God's omnipresence does not prevent sin, disease, death, lack, and limitation from continuing. Knowing that God is all does not stop the process or the progress of sin, disease, death, lack, and limitation. Knowing that God is closer than breathing does not do it, nor does knowing that God is omnipotence and omnipresence do it.

What then is necessary? What is the something beyond the intellectual knowledge of God? If the truth of God as omnipresence, omnipotence, and omniscience could be *realized*—not mentally stated or agreed with, but realized— that is all that would be necessary for the establishment of harmony in our being. But it is so rare that an individual ever attains the realization that God is all to any demonstrable degree that you would probably have difficulty remembering the names of three persons since the time of Christ Jesus who have attained it. Yet, it is true that the realization that God is all is sufficient for our every need.

Inasmuch, however, as this truth of the allness of God has not been realized to a great enough degree by enough people of the world, there must be something to be learned in addition to that, some principle or law, or some way that will make it possible for us to realize God's allness and thereby overcome sin, disease, death, lack, and limitation within ourselves and within those who turn to us.

## *The Impersonal Origin of Evil*

One of the most important of the principles revealed to me was the impersonal cause and nature of evil. All evil, regardless of its name or nature, is impersonal. That means that it is not your wrong thinking that has caused your trouble—not your envy, jealousy, or malice, not your sensuality, your lack of gratitude, not your anything. Not a single thing in you is responsible for any of your ills. By seeking within yourself or within your patient for the cause of the trouble, you are helping to perpetuate it and making it almost impossible for healing to be brought about. The evil or error that is finding expression in you, whether as a disease, an evil trait of character, or as a false appetite, has absolutely nothing to do with you. It did not begin in you, and you will never root it out of you. You never will.

Evil has its origin in something that for the moment we may call the carnal mind. If the term "carnal mind" means nothing to you, call it Satan. If these terms do not appeal to you, call it an appearance, a claim, or an illusion. The name you give it is unimportant. The important thing is to know that evil, of whatever name or nature, stems from a universal impersonal source.

Unless you can separate evil from the individual, separate it so completely that even if you saw a man stealing a pocketbook, you could say to yourself, "Thank God, I know you are not a thief. The carnal mind is behind this"—unless you can do this, there is not the remotest possibility of your healing anyone.

If you are confronted with a case of cancer, and are tempted to believe that jealousy, hatred, or sensuality has caused it or any other condition or circumstance, you have little hope of success as a healer. Even if you do heal someone occasionally, such a healing probably came about more or less accidentally or because you caught some absolute statement of truth which made you rise higher than your own beliefs. The truth is that there are no human qualities that cause cancer or any other disease. Cancers have been found in newborn babies, and certainly there is nothing hateful, sensual, or jealous about them. And furthermore, there are some mighty fine, pure men and women in the world who have suffered from serious diseases who never knew such a thing as hate, sensuality, or jealousy to any great extent.

You must instantly impersonalize every claim by realizing that it has its origin in an impersonal source. Whether you call it carnal mind or an appearance makes no difference, but whatever you do, be sure you understand that it is not in your patient or in your student or, above all things, in yourself. The reason you can have that assurance is that God constitutes your identity. Your name is *I*. That you call yourself *I* is evidence of that. The only way you can identify yourself is as *I*, and that *I* is your identity, but that *I* also is God. *I* has no evil qualities or propensities.

True, there may be times when you and I feel beset by some of the evil rampant in the world. We may feel hatred or envy or even entertain wicked thoughts. But that is just a part of the universal mesmerism, and we must not condemn ourselves. It has been picked up out of the ether, and has no relationship to us because the minute we know that we are *I*, we will know that we have no evil qualities, propensities, or characteristics, and any of these that seem to be a part of us are but the projection of that which we call carnal mind or Satan, meaning the impersonal source of evil.

### All Evil Stems from the Belief in Two Powers

When you have reached this point and are able to do this, half your battle is won, but only half. The next step is a bitter pill to swallow because now you have to recognize that St. Paul made a serious mistake, a mistake that has helped to keep us in bondage and has been fatal to the world. He suffered for years, all because of his erroneous conclusion in regard to the carnal mind. It is true that he did impersonalize. It is true that he did not blame anyone for his troubles: he did not say it was because of the Romans or the Greeks or the Jews. He knew it was the carnal mind. But what he did not know was that the carnal mind is not enmity against God.

The carnal mind is the "arm of flesh," nothingness. The carnal mind is a belief in two powers. And wherever, or to whatever extent, the belief in two powers exists, there is carnal mind. Some persons are less hypnotized by this belief than others, but there is no one on earth who is completely free of the belief in good and evil. Complete freedom comes only after the resurrection.

Those of us on the metaphysical path, however, have in a measure, already come out of the belief in good and evil. For example, there are probably few persons reading this book who would not immediately answer a call to a case of infectious or contagious disease without any fear that they would take on the contagion or infection. And that is because everyone on this path has already gone far enough to know that since God is the only power, infection and contagion are nothing but a belief of two powers.

On the other hand, if we were to learn this afternoon that there might be an atomic bomb dropped on us tonight, we probably would not have quite that unconcern. It might be more difficult for us to say, "Well, what of it? If God is the only power, I can't see what difference it makes if bombs are dropped all around me." Actually, that should be the attitude of every person on the spiritual path because where he is, God is.

When Hezekiah, king of Judah, learned that Sennacherib, king of Assyria, was encamped against him and his people, he gathered together his captains "and spake comfortably to them, saying, ... with him is an arm of flesh; but with us is the Lord our God to help us."⁴ What he really was saying was, "We have all-might, and they have none. Their numbers do not constitute power. Their weapons do not constitute power because God is all-power; therefore numbers and weapons are not power."

If you are of those who believe that an atomic bomb is power, then you are in the midst of the only error that can come into your life: the belief in two powers. To the degree that you accept the belief in two powers, good and evil, in that degree are you the victim, not of two powers, because there are not two powers, but the victim of the *belief* in two powers. If you can but become convinced that the origin of evil is the universal belief in two powers, you will have the basic secret of life, that which the ancients sought, and which some of them discovered but found they were unable to teach mankind.

### Becoming Free of the Belief in Two Powers

The understanding and conviction that there are not two powers is not easy to achieve. How many people are there in all the world who are not subject to the belief in good and evil? Are we not all in a measure under the hypnotism of this belief? Is not even a child under that belief from the moment of conception?

The only way a child can be freed from this hypnotism is if his parents, before his conception, have become aware of the truth that neither the mind of man nor the body of man is a creator. God alone is the creator, and God is the one and only power, and all creation is subject unto God alone. With a realized consciousness of this truth, parents will then bring forth a child free of this belief in two powers, and that child will function as a beloved son of God, free from the world beliefs about infants' and children's diseases and problems.

If this could be a continuing realization, there would be no problem of old age. In dealing with the problems of those who are suffering from world beliefs regarding the calendar and its effects, it is necessary to go beyond merely repeating that harmony is a realization of the mesmeric nature of that which appears as senility, weakness, and deterioration, all of which the world accepts as signs or evidences of advancing years. It is necessary to understand that these appearances are but pictures produced by the hypnotic influence of the belief in two powers. To understand this is to dispel, in a measure, the appearance, and to reveal the Christ-nature which is ageless, birthless, and deathless.

Any appearance of age, regardless of whether it comes at fifty or at ninety, should be treated as a mesmeric appearance, having no foundation in God, no spiritual authorization or ordination, and therefore, no entity or identity. Always remember that it is more important to know and understand the nature of error than, parrot-like, to repeat that God is all.

Evil exists only as a belief in two powers, a universal belief, never your belief, never his belief, never its belief—just a belief. This belief in two powers, which we call the carnal mind, is not a power, and it is not a cause. It is the "arm of flesh" or nothingness. It is a belief, an illusion, an appearance; but it has no reality and it has no law because it is not God-ordained.

God never created two powers, and God never created a belief in two powers. Therefore, that belief has no God-ordination and no God-power. It is not a cause and has no law to maintain it or sustain it. All that is required to be free of the belief in two powers is to know the truth, and the truth to know is that what God did not create was not made or empowered. Since the belief in good and evil is not God-made, it is not God-ordained or God-sustained, and has no law of God to perpetuate it.

The first step in our healing work is to impersonalize the evil—remove it from the person—and never be guilty of saying it is "he," "she," or "it," but always remove the error into the universal carnal mind. Then when you take the second step of declaring that this carnal mind is not enmity against God, that it is a belief without God, without law, without presence, and without power to sustain it, you will find that you have accomplished seventy-five to eighty per cent of your healing work.

In at least seventy-five to eighty per cent of all our cases, healing should be accomplished quickly and completely. Whatever the name or nature of the case, it does not have its foundation in anything for which the patient is responsible, and by recognizing the universal impersonal nature of it and its impotency, it is removed. Actually, it is not removed, but this clearer vision sees the eternal perfection that has always existed right where the apparent discord was.

For example, nobody is responsible for having the flu. You cannot blame a person or look within him to find the qualities that brought that disease upon him. It is just something flying around in the atmosphere, and he picks it up. Therefore, when one person recognizes that any such epidemic is a universal belief, not personal to anybody, and that it has no law of God sustaining it, he has stopped it; and he may have experiences such as I had when that realization was so complete that every case that came to my office in a whole day was met on the day it came to me without ever thinking about a patient or being concerned as to who called or when. Just holding to the realization that whatever call came to me was nothing but a claim of a selfhood, a law, or an activity apart from God, and was not personal and so not power, but only the "arm of flesh" or nothingness, took care of every situation.

Seventy-five or eighty per cent of all the claims that afflict individuals are very quickly met through this method of treatment. The difficulty lies with the other twenty per cent of which the Master said, "Howbeit this kind goeth not out but by prayer and fasting."[5] A practitioner has to rise high in consciousness to meet some of those cases. If my own experience is any criterion, no one meets all of them. But a great number of them can be met, and we can come to a point where we are meeting ninety to ninety-five per cent of all the cases that come to us. For the rest, we have to go still higher before we can attain the consciousness that will meet them.

### Protective Work

There is a step beyond the healing of disease, and that lies in the area of preventing the ills of the flesh from ever coming into our experience. Through an activity of consciousness we, individually, can escape ninety or more per cent of all the evils that beset the world. We can live a life almost completely free of lack and limitation, no matter to what extent lack and limitation may be experienced by the rest of the world. We can live in health, regardless of the extent to which disease and epidemics stalk up and down the world.

None of these things will come nigh our dwelling place, but this freedom can be demonstrated only through the understanding and application of specific principles. This we call protective work, not that we protect ourselves from any people, race, or religion, or that we protect ourselves from any sins or diseases. Far be it from such. The meaning of protective work is protecting ourselves from the acceptance of these universal beliefs.

This subject of protective work is dealt with specifically in the chapters entitled "Protection" in *The 1955 Infinite Way Letters*,[6] and "Break the Fetters That Bind You" in *The 1958 Infinite Way Letters*.[7] From a study of these two chapters, you will learn that you wake up every morning to "this world," the world governed by laws of matter and laws of mind, all based on two powers. You must consciously remove yourself from this world of two powers, and come out and be separate. There is no power outside of you that will do this for you, and until, through an act of consciousness, you do it for yourself, life will go on eternally presenting problems of one kind or another to you. You must consciously free yourself from these human laws and place yourself under grace. This has to be done every day. There is no one who has become sufficiently advanced to omit this daily conscious realization:

*Since I am I, I am not under the law, but under grace. Since I am I, there are no laws external to me acting upon me. I am the law, and I am the dominion unto "this world."*

This is the truth, but if you do not make it an activity of your consciousness, you do not bring it to pass in your experience, and you cannot demonstrate it.

God as individual being, the impersonalization of evil in the realization that it has no person on whom or through whom to operate, and the "nothingization" of all evil as having no God-ordination—these principles constitute the truth that makes you free.

## ACROSS THE DESK

To the enlightened, there is no death, no separation, no end. New Jerusalem is here, and now. While it is natural to miss those who make this transition called death, especially those with whom we have had close ties and long companionship, let us understand death so that our grief may not be too long, or too deep.

Every birth ultimately eventuates in death, and knowing this should prepare us for that experience when it comes to our loved ones or to ourselves. At birth, there is no guarantee of the length of the individual human span. It may be more than the traditional threescore years and ten, or much less. This is known at birth, so why should we be shocked and grief-stricken when death occurs?

As to death itself: Know ye not that there is no death, that this is a transitional experience which must come to all?

Know ye not that life becomes a burden on earth when one's work is done, or when daily living includes nothing more than eating, sleeping, and wasting time in pastimes and pleasure?

Know ye not that when an individual stops serving and giving and doing that he has already died even though he still occupies space on earth?

Know ye not that life is loving, and when one ceases to love, to give, to share, and to spend oneself, he has already died even though he be still visible to us?

Know ye not that when one no longer learns, death has already come even while still walking on earth? If every day does not add knowledge, wisdom, power, the ability to live life and the capacity to love, we have already died. Let us not hold ourselves or others in bondage to breathing without a purpose or goal. Rather let us seek the far country.

Do not grieve. Rather rejoice that a new experience is about to begin, one which includes greater opportunities to serve, to learn, to give, and to be.

The tree that no longer bears fruit is withered and ready to be cut down. The man who no longer gives the fruit of labor and love is likewise withered.

Death is really not the end of life, but rather the beginning of the rebirthed life. Rejoice to see it, and bless the traveler on his new journey. Release the departing traveler and give him as a Godspeed a flower lei of happy memories and a benediction as he migrates to the promised land, the far country—New Jerusalem.

## ❖ 4 ❖

# CHRIST RAISED FROM THE TOMB

THE HEBREWS OF OLD foresaw the coming of the Messiah, but because they believed that the Messiah would be some kind of great king or general, someone who could lead them to victory over Caesar or perhaps even over their own Sanhedrin, a man who would turn the evil conditions of their day into good conditions, they were unable to accept the gentle Master. Instead of understanding that "My kingdom" is not of this world, they accepted the God of the Forty-seventh Psalm:

> O clap your hands, all ye people; shout unto God with the voice of triumph.
>
> For the Lord most high is terrible; he is a great King over all the earth.
>
> He shall subdue the people under us, and the nations under our feet.

From the time of the Hebrews under Pharaoh unto this very day, the same prayer has gone up, the same psalms have been sung, and the same hope expressed that God will subdue nations, remove tyrants, and overcome the armies of the aliens. Should not thousands of years of such praying have proved that God has done none of these things up to now, and that there is no likelihood of his doing them at any future date?

In the Forty-sixth Psalm there is an indication that the nature of God has been misunderstood, and that that is one reason peace on earth and good will to men have not been experienced.

God is our refuge and strength, a very present help in trouble.

Therefore will not we fear, though the earth be removed, and though the mountains be carried into the midst of the sea;

Though the waters thereof roar and be troubled, though the mountains shake with the swelling thereof.

There is a river, the streams whereof shall make glad the city of God, the holy place of the tabernacles of the most High.

God is in the midst of her; she shall not be moved: God shall help her, and that right early.

The heathen raged, the kingdoms were moved: he uttered his voice, the earth melted.

The Lord of hosts is with us; the God of Jacob is our refuge.

Come, behold the works of the Lord, what desolations he hath made in the earth.

He maketh wars to cease unto the end of the earth; he breaketh the bow, and cutteth the spear in sunder; he burneth the chariot in the fire.

Be still, and know that I am God: I will be exalted among the heathen, I will be exalted in the earth.

The Lord of hosts is with us; the God of Jacob is our refuge.

The greater part of this Psalm refers to God as our refuge and strength, and therefore, will we not fear. It is up to us; not to God—to us. We will not fear, because God is our refuge. If we can gain an understanding of the nature of God and of the Messiah or the Christ, we shall find that earthly conditions dissolve, and that harmony can be brought into our experience, not only as individuals, but as a united world because God is no respecter of persons, of religions, or of races. God is one, and God is equally the Father of us all. When God is known, understood, and contacted, that presence does change the course of our human experience.

### *Turn Away from the Worship of Personality*

The belief that the Christ was a man and the worship of the Christ as a person have blinded the eyes of mankind to the truth that God is spirit, God is love, and God is life. God is not a man, and it is not a man that is to accomplish these great things on earth.

We must never place our faith in a man or in a book. Many persons have placed their entire faith in the idea that the Bible is a holy book, but the Bible of itself has no power. It is the truth that is revealed in the Bible that does the work, not the book, but the revealed truth of Scripture. When this truth becomes a part of our consciousness, we are knowing the truth, and as we assimilate the truths of Scripture and as they become a living part of our being, we are able to demonstrate: first, that God is; next, that God is closer than breathing; and then, that God takes over our experience.

At first, we may prove only that God takes over the experience of our personal lives. In other words, as a person seeks for God, for truth, or for reality, and as he becomes somewhat aware of this presence that is already within him, miracles begin to take place in his experience: changes in health, in human relationships, and in other areas. A greater sense of safety and security comes to him, a greater inner peace, all of which are reflected in his outer life.

As this continues, it then becomes apparent that whatever it is that is taking place in this person is also in some measure touching the members of his family. He is beginning to bring more peace into his household. It very soon becomes evident that a new influence has come into the home, that something has taken place in the outer experience which indicates what has taken place in the inner life of one or more individuals of that household.

This is then noticed by neighbors, friends, and relatives, and eventually those in far places begin to be aware of this spiritual stirring, even without knowing what it is that is happening. So we find that one individual, a Moses, for example, will lead an entire people out of slavery into some measure of freedom and law. A Jesus will not only begin to reveal the nature of spiritual freedom to his immediate people, but down through two thousand years, untold numbers of persons will be touched by that same spirit that was awakened in this Hebrew rabbi who became the Christ, and that very spirit will be felt in the consciousness of individuals, even as it is felt today and will be for all days to come.

Millions of people are now receiving spiritual light, inner peace, and outer harmony through the spirit that has been revealed by great mystics like Lao-Tze, Gautama the Buddha, Shankara, Guru Nanak, and others who have become illumined by the revelation of a divine presence and power within.

The secret of all of these mystics has been their discovery of God and the Christ, and in the teachings of every one of them is found the admonition not to worship the individual. Jesus said, "I can of mine own self do nothing ... If I bear witness of myself, my witness is not true.[1] ... My doctrine is not mine, but his that sent me.[2] ... The Father that dwelleth in me, he doeth the works."[3] What is Jesus doing but turning us away from personality to the realization and revelation of the spirit? So it has always been with the great illumined souls of the world. Each one has turned his followers away from personality to the revealed truth of an inner presence—an inner presence found not only in Moses, Elijah, Elisha, Isaiah, Jesus, Paul, and John, but a presence within every living thing.

Occasionally statements such as "Be still, and know that I am God: I will be exalted among the heathen, I will be exalted in the earth,"[4] reveal to us our true identity, the nature of God, and the nature of the Messiah or the Christ. If we are wise and sufficiently discerning, such inspired passages may reveal all the secrets necessary for us to know.

As the human race, we are the heathen. It makes no difference whether we are a little more of heathen, as some are, or a little less, as some others are; as the human race, we are nevertheless the heathen until one glorious moment of revelation.

## Being Reborn

Paul explained very clearly that "the natural man receiveth not the things of the spirit of God."[5] The natural man, that is, the human man, is not under God's grace or under God's government. "But ye are not in the flesh, but in the spirit, if so be that the spirit of God dwell in you."[6] *If, if, if* so be, *when* the spirit of God dwells in you. Ah, there is the secret!

As we continue our study of the spiritual wisdom of the world, we shall discover, as it was revealed in the Christian message and thousands of years before, that the object of our search for God is to "die" that we may be reborn. Mortality must be put off, and immortality be put on.

The whole secret of the spiritual teaching of the world is that the heathen in us must "die" in order that the son of God may be raised up in us. As human beings, we are the tomb in which the Christ is buried. As human beings, referred to by the Master in the fifteenth chapter of John, we are the branch of a tree that is cut off and withers and dies. This is the heathen; this is the human; but when the branch is one with the vine, then do we bear fruit richly. Why? Because we are permitting the Christ to live in us, and we are living in the Christ. Now we have moved from our heathenhood to our Christhood, from being a natural man to being that man in whom the spirit of God dwells.

Saul of Tarsus expresses clearly the state of consciousness of the human being intellectually and religiously taught, the good man humanly, the ardent seeker of God humanly, and yet a persecutor of that which he was seeking. When Saul of Tarsus "died," or was stricken "blind," his eyes were opened, and the "death" of Saul became the "birth" of St. Paul. This symbolizes the "death" of that natural man *seeking* the kingdom of God, and the "birth" of the spiritual man who has *realized* the kingdom of God.

Since the Master spent his entire ministry revealing that the kingdom of God is not in holy mountains or holy temples but is within us, if we are to "die" to our heathenhood and be reborn of the spirit, we must realize that whatever change is to take place in us is not going to come about because we go to some holy place or find some holy man or holy book. The change is going to take place if we will permit that holy place, holy temple, holy man, or holy book to reveal to us that the spirit of God is within us and must be revealed within our own being, so that we accept it as a personal responsibility to seek until we find, knock until the door is opened to us, and we are able to hear:

I *in the midst of you am mighty.* I *in the midst of you am God;* I *in the midst of you will be exalted in the earth when you recognize* Me *within you, when you recognize that the spirit of God dwelleth in you, when you realize that the son of God is hidden in that tomb that you call "you."*

## The Dark Night of the Soul

Saul of Tarsus, the Prodigal Son, the woman taken in adultery, the thief on the cross—what are these but you and me? They represent the tomb in which the Christ is buried; they represent the mortality of human life. It makes no difference for the moment whether we are an earnest seeker as was Saul of Tarsus, the sinning woman, or the pleasure-seeking prodigal. The reference is still to us, to our human nature, to the mortal side of us, and in that very mortality is buried this Christ, this son of God which must be lifted up, exalted, and recognized. When that Christ is recognized, then what happens? We become still:

*"Speak, Lord; for thy servant heareth."[7] I will be still that I may hear thy voice. I will be still that this spirit in me may utter its voice.*

This spirit is not floating around in the air; this spirit is not sitting upon a cloud: this spirit that is to utter its voice is within us. The kingdom of God, the allness, the realm of God is within us, but then also the reign of God!

As we learn through our meditations to be at peace, to be receptive and responsive to this that is within us, eventually we, too, will have an experience. I realize, of course, that the vast majority of our students do not enjoy the experience when it comes. Perhaps that is because they would all like it to come peaceably, gently, sweetly, and gradually, but this is not the way it has come to most of those who have experienced it. It usually comes as a blinding experience; it often is a very distressing and disturbing period. For Paul and for every mystic it has been a terrible experience! It is called the dark night of the Soul, and it would be comforting if there were only one such night.

Unfortunately, there are many dark nights leading up to the experience of being "blinded," being "stricken dead," or being "mortally wounded." But when we are helpless and hopeless, when there is not a trace of human strength or power left in us, or human wisdom, when we have come to that place of unknowing, when there is no possibility of our having any human ability to help ourselves, in that moment the voice speaks within and says,

*Know ye not, I am in the midst of thee, and I am thy God. I am thy bread, and thy meat, and thy wine, and thy water. I am the resurrection, restoring unto you even the lost years of the locust. I am your life eternal.*

### The Nature and Function of the Christ

Now perhaps we can begin to perceive the nature of the Christ. The Christ is not a great king; the Christ is not a general. The Christ does not conquer nations militarily or politically. The Christ conquers nations through its gentle spirit, because when the loud noise is over, when the destructive period is past—the dark night of the Soul—this that is within us begins to reveal itself in humble and gentle ways, leading us step by step from the discords and inharmonies of human existence to the higher attitude and altitude of spiritual living and into spiritual grace.

The first evidence of the Christ in our experience is an improvement in our human affairs. Our nature, our disposition, our health, even the amount of our supply, and certainly a greater harmony in our human relationships: these are the first signs of the raised-up son of God in us. All these changes, however, are only steps, because the ultimate of spiritual revelation lies in this statement: "My kingdom is not of this world."[8]

When harmony has been restored, then begins the second and final stage in which we are lifted above physical and mental harmony, above all the harmonies of this world, and begin to perceive the nature of spiritual grace. The function of the Christ is to reveal to us a spiritual kingdom far greater than a human world with good government, or even human beings who are kind instead of unkind to one another. Right here on earth, a new universe, a new mode of life is revealed to us.

Always the disciple is instructed not to leave this world, but to remain in it, to be in it, yes, but not of it. We walk through life eating the same kind of food, making use of the same modes of transportation, and operating the same businesses or engaging in the same arts and sciences, but with this difference: we do it now not for a living, but for the joy of action, for the joy of being.

Try now to make a transition in your understanding of the nature of the Christ. Perhaps you have been delaying your own spiritual progress by thinking that this Christ has the function of removing your bodily diseases, providing you with a larger income, with a promotion, or something else of a human nature. Sometimes we even think that it ought to settle our traffic tickets, or other things of a similar nature. But God is not to be used; the Christ is not to be used. It is not something to which we can turn in the expectation that it will do something for us. No, the Christ is that into which we relax ourselves, not that it may do something in our lives, but that it may be our life.

As human beings, all we think of is what we would like our life to be, and we aim our thoughts toward the Christ with a preconceived idea of what we would like it to do for us or in us, whereas the real function of the Christ is to lead us to a point where we "die," where we become completely "dead" to that life that we have been trying to glorify, so that the *I*, the spirit within us, may be exalted, but not so that we may take pride and boast, "Oh, look what God is doing for me." There is no God to do anything *for* me or *for you*. God is infinite being, and God lives unto God. God lives unto itself, manifested as individual being, but never, never departing from its own life.

### *Personal Selfhood*
### *Must Be Surrendered*

"The heavens declare the glory of God; and the firmament sheweth his handywork."[9] Man is here not to be glorified, but that God may be glorified; and God is glorified only in the degree that we surrender this personal sense of life and come to the ultimate revelation as given by Paul: "I live; yet not I, but Christ liveth in me."[10] In that state of consciousness, there is a surrender of personal selfhood, a surrender of the desire to get God to do something to us, or through us, or for us, such a surrender that it lets God live his life as us. Now there is no more room for self-glory, *I* will be exalted, not *I* will exalt *you*. *I* will be exalted—God will be exalted. God will be lifted up, and God will live his life on earth as God lives his life in heaven. In other words, the spirit of God fills all space in heaven above, on earth, and beneath the earth. We need only to realize that it is God living God's life, not God performing something for us.

This is the big barrier. All of the prayers of wanting God to do something for us, for our nation, to do something against our enemies, or to make us more successful than our competitors: this is the barrier. God is life, and since there is no life but God, we must surrender our false sense of life until God becomes our very life, and then let God live it.

Do you see why the ancient Hebrews failed to understand the function of the Messiah? They expected this Messiah to go out and destroy somebody or something for them. God does not overcome any enemies outside of us, but he does overcome the enemies within us; and in reality the only enemies we have are those within our own nature, that part of us which constitutes our humanhood.

The idea of self-preservation at the expense of any and all has become such a dominant characteristic of human beings that it is called the first law of nature. This is the most evil part of our nature and that is the enemy within which must be overcome. I cannot ask God to overcome it within you; I have to ask God to overcome it within me. If I have a trace of self-preservation or if I have a trace of desire for something other than what I also desire for you, that is the enemy, the false sense of self within me which must be overcome.

If there is such a thing as God being the Father, and all men the sons of that Father, how inconsistent it is to invoke the aid of God *for* one and *against* another! The secret of the ancient schools of wisdom was that the initiate was to be trained, instructed, and enlightened until he came to the full awareness of himself as the spiritual child of God. There was no teaching about using this power to do something to somebody else, or for somebody else: it was purely one of self-development, self-realization, in order to bring each one to that point where the son of God could be raised from the tomb. But it was not taught that the tomb is in Jerusalem: the tomb is our human selfhood, the human mind, the human consciousness, the false sense of self. That is the tomb in which the Christ is buried.

## *The Work of the*
## *Initiate Is Enlightenment*

Until our own blindness and inadequacy have been removed, we are not the light of the world; but if we can forget the world for a moment and concentrate on our own self-enlightenment, very soon we shall discover that even the small measure of light that we have become is already having an effect upon our families. As this light grows and grows and as we become more spiritually aware, it touches the lives of friends and neighbors, and as we have seen in this work, it is beginning to affect people in every part of the globe and on every continent. The illumined consciousness of just one, two, or ten is making itself felt in a world-wide way. In other words, the smallest possible group of spiritually enlightened people can save this entire world from destruction, but how futile for anyone in his blindness to try to lead someone else!

Where the spirit of the Lord is, there is peace, there is harmony, there is justice. It does not mean that there have to be ten thousand people: it means that there has to be the spirit of the Lord, and that spirit of the Lord is right here where we are. As a matter of fact, the spirit of the Lord is wherever the spirit of the Lord is realized. There is no way to confine the spirit of the Lord once it has been released from consciousness. Has not the spirit of the Lord, when released through the Master, continued to operate in consciousness down through the ages? No number of years has been able to stop the operation of the spirit of the Lord in the consciousness of those who have opened themselves to it.

Therefore, the first step is your enlightenment and mine that we may individually raise up this son of God in us, and in some measure "die" to the struggle for self-preservation. As we perceive that God's grace is a universal grace, we begin to understand that it is not self-preservation that matters because this is only a law of human nature, and human nature is the tomb of the Christ. The real spiritual law is that we be willing to lay down our life for a friend, to lay down our life for our neighbor, to lay down this human sense of life in order that even the least of our brothers may be raised up, that we be willing to let this false sense of life disappear from us that the Christ-life may appear, and in that Christ-life serve mankind as Jesus did by leading generations of people to an awareness of the spiritual nature of life.

This is not using God, this is not using truth: this is surrendering our personal sense of life in order that we may be used, that we may be a transparency through which God's grace can touch the life of all mankind. The purpose of this search for God, of the initiate's undertaking the work of enlightenment, of our being on the spiritual path, is that we may lose our life, surrender this personal sense of life, be clothed upon with immortality, and be a transparency through which the grace of God may reach this earth and overcome the kingdom of men's minds. It is not the kingdom of men's governments that is to be overcome, not the kingdom of his politics; it is not even his armies that are to be overcome: it is the mind and its iniquity that must be overcome; it is the enemy within our own household, our mental household, that is to be overcome. The Christ is the law of elimination, working through love to overcome the enemy within ourselves.

### The Christ Destroys the Enemy Within

Follow the Master for a moment into the wilderness where he was tempted. Do you see that it was the evil within himself that was tempting him, and that he was saying unto the evil, " 'Get thee behind me, Satan!'[11] I cannot be tempted, for I am not here to glorify myself, but that God may be glorified. If I perform a miracle to glorify myself, I will have lost the kingdom of God. Get thee behind me!"

Then when his consciousness was made free of personal sense, personal glorification, self-preservation, he could go forward and fulfill his ministry because now he could not be tempted by anything external to himself. He had overcome the world when the enemy within his gates had been overcome, and the enemy within his gates was the mortal sense of selfhood that sought to preserve itself, instead of wanting to let itself "die" in order that the *I* might be exalted, that the spirit of God in him might be the light of the world.

When there was no longer any personal sense left, when the Master was no longer living his own life, he had the capacity to heal the sick, to raise the dead, to forgive the sinner, and to feed the hungry because then he knew that his finite capacities were of no importance whatsoever and were not to be relied upon. He had no small capacities or great capacities: he had no capacities, period. He was the transparency for the divine capacity, the spiritual, the infinite, the *all*-capacity.

The kingdom of God is within you and me, and the function of the Christ is to purify you and me. We are not to call upon the Christ to do something to someone else, but we are to realize that the Christ is functioning in human consciousness to dispel personal sense, first in us, in our friends, and then in our enemies. Let us pray for the enemy that we may be children of God, pray the prayer of realization that the kingdom of God be just as much in our enemy as in our friend, awaiting only this recognition to be brought up from the tomb, raised again, and resurrected into life eternal.

Rightly to understand the nature of the Christ, we must begin to perceive that it is not going out into the world to destroy our enemies. It is to be admitted into our consciousness to destroy the enemies within ourselves. These enemies are made up of all phases of personal sense from the greatest evil, self-preservation, to the least evil which is believing that we are good, philanthropic, religious, spiritual, or moral, which we are not, and cannot be, for only the presence of God in us is good. When we lose our sense of evil and later lose our sense of good, then we are a clear transparency through which the grace of God can shine upon this world—upon our own families and friends first, and gradually, as the circle widens, it will embrace the whole world.

# ✣ 5 ✣

## WITHINNESS

WHEN A PERSON COMES into some measure of understanding of the nature of God, a change takes place in his life. This coming to know God aright is often referred to as illumination, and as illumination changes consciousness from a limited sense to one of infinitely greater capacity, a new life begins to unfold.

Even a faint glimpse of the real nature of God brings an understanding of the Master's revelation that the kingdom of God is neither lo here, nor lo there, but is within. With that recognition, vital changes begin to take place in your life, and perhaps the most important of these is that you are no longer consumed by fear. What is there to fear if there is a God? What could be a power over God? What could harm God? Is there a power greater than God?

To believe that there is a power greater than God is atheism. It is to have no God, because the only God there is, is omnipotence, omnipresence, omniscience. Therefore, when you have a God that is all-power, that is present wherever you are, and that is infinite intelligence, what is there to fear? How could disease or lack or limitation be present? How could death enter into the presence of all-power, all-presence, and all-wisdom?

Those who live in the realization of God as omnipotence, omnipresence, and omniscience are free of the pitfalls that come nigh the dwelling place of those who do not dwell in the secret place of the most High. This does not mean simply going to church or belonging to a church, as this does not keep a person from being an atheist. The only thing that separates anyone from atheism is an actual conviction of God. Joining an organization does not do it. In fact, it is possible to join the noblest and loftiest of movements and yet not take on the nature of its teaching. A person can be a member of a fraternal lodge founded upon the most high-minded principles and still go on cheating and defrauding, but this he could not do if he had an understanding and conviction of the real meaning underlying the teaching of that fraternal order.

It is possible to join a church and still be fundamentally an atheist. Atheists can be found inside and outside the church. On the other hand, a person is a theist if he has never belonged to a church as long as he has attained a conviction of God, and not only a conviction that God is, but that God is wherever he is, omnipresent.

### *No Power from Without Can Operate Upon You*

When you are convinced that the place whereon you stand is holy ground, you are no longer in fear—even if bombs should burst, for not even being blown to bits can separate you from life.

If it is true that the kingdom of God is within you, no power external to you can operate in your life. No evil power can act upon you, in you, or through you because the kingdom of God within you would immediately dissolve any such power, if there were one. Nothing from without your being can enter to defile or make a lie—no external power, no external force, whether of the nature of sin, disease, or of lack—nothing, absolutely nothing. That is your protection.

You may wonder, then, why so much evil, so much sin, disease, lack, limitation, and even death have come into your experience, but if you are on the spiritual path, you must acknowledge that these discords have not come to you from without. There is no way to make spiritual progress, to bring about purification, no way to put off mortality and put on immortality without first recognizing that no power of evil has ever entered your experience from outside your own being.

When you have acknowledged this, your next step is to find out what it is within your own being that is responsible for the sin, disease, or accidents that have come into your experience. Eventually, it is borne in upon you that what is responsible for the ills of mankind is darkness, ignorance—ignorance of truth. The Master promised, "Ye shall know the truth, and the truth shall make you free."[1] It must be plain, therefore, that if you are not free it is because of your lack of knowing the truth, and this, of course, means because of your ignorance.

Ignorance is responsible for your ills, but fortunately ignorance is something you can do something about. If there were a devil or a Satan external to you, responsible for your ills, you might be justified in saying, "There is nothing I can do about it but suffer it"; or if the stars and the planets possessed power to govern your life, you might also say, "I can do nothing about that." If there were conditions external to yourself that could be held responsible for your ills, you could protest, "Well, I can do nothing about them. I must bear them." But the Master declared, "Ye shall know the truth, and the truth shall make you free."

Paul went further than that when he said, "Whatsoever a man soweth, that shall he also reap."[2] He did not hesitate to lay your problems right on your own doorstep, and he added, "He that soweth to his flesh shall of the flesh reap corruption; but he that soweth to the spirit shall of the spirit reap life everlasting."[3] And so again it is you—you.

But this does not mean that you are condemned, or that you should condemn yourself. Since Jesus did not condemn anyone, but in every case, even to those who had sinned, his response was, "Neither do I condemn thee,"[4] you will realize that you are not under condemnation even for your ignorance. You have within sow. God is not responsible for your ills; God is not responsible for your death. "For I have no pleasure in the death of him that dieth, saith the Lord God: wherefore turn yourselves, and live ye."[5]

### Forgiveness Is at the Instant of Repentance

Above all things, if any one of you is living in fear that God is punishing you for some sin, lose that fear in this hour, for it is not true. God has never punished anyone for any sin. There is no provision in God for punishment of any nature. According to the teachings of the Master, forgiveness is unto seventy times seven. What about the 491st time? It never comes. It would not be possible to forgive and forgive and forgive without bringing healing to the one you are forgiving. What the Master really meant was that forgiveness should continue until a healing takes place, forgive until there is nothing left to be forgiven, but never condemn, never judge.

Although a person is punished for and by his sins, he is punished only so long as the sins continue. The very moment that he looks up and turns away from them, in that moment, though his sins be scarlet, he is white as snow, and he does not have to wait for death to give him the forgiveness he is seeking. His forgiveness is at the instant of his turning, at the instant of his repentance.

Do not accept the belief that the discord from which you are suffering is of God, or that God is the author or the cause of your suffering—not even for a good reason, for there is no good reason ever revealed by the Master. The Master's whole teaching is one of forgiveness, and when you can come into agreement within yourself that God is not the author of your discords or inharmonies, of your mental, physical, moral, or financial troubles, you have taken a great step forward and have released yourself from the belief that God is holding you in bondage.

### Accept Your God-Given Dominion

The realization that there is no power outside of your own being responsible for your ills prepares you for the next step, which is to understand that the suffering, the lack, and the limitation in your life are due to something within you, not to something outside of you, and that there is nobody in heaven, on earth, or in hell responsible for this condition. The fault which must be corrected is nothing but ignorance of the truth, and that you can do something about. You never have suffered and never will suffer from anything other than ignorance of truth, and that you can correct at any time.

*All power is within me. God gave me dominion over all that is in the earth and in the skies above the earth, including the stars and the planets and their astrological implications.*

*God gave man dominion. Therefore, all dominion, all law and all power—is within me. It is not mine in a personal or an egotistical sense as though it were of my own self. It is mine by the grace of God. God gave me this dominion; God gave me this power over all beliefs of power. God instilled his dominion in my consciousness from the very beginning. God-given dominion is my dominion over all the forces that exist.*

When you have a feeling within you that this is the truth, you begin to perceive that you need not take up the sword against any external powers because he that lives by the sword will die by the sword. You begin to understand why the Master said, "Resist not evil,"[6] why he never set up a warfare against the devil, and why he never battled evil. There is no record of his fighting the devil, no record of his warring with Satan, but merely a quiet, peaceful, "Get thee behind me."[7] And we hear no more of the devil in the Master's life.

You, too, have God-given dominion over all the devils that may torment or tempt you. Always you have dominion, but that dominion is exercised only by the recognition of the truth that makes you free. You do not have to battle; you do not have to struggle; you have to know the truth:

*There is a God-given dominion within me. The kingdom of God is within me, and this kingdom of God within me is the law; it is the son of God; it is the presence of God that is within each and every individual.*

*God has given me dominion over all that is, and this God-given dominion within me is now operating to free me, whether it is of sin, lack, disease, hate, envy, jealousy, or of resentment.*

*This God-given dominion is operative now within me. The kingdom of God within me is jurisdiction and dominion over everything there is in this world.*

Although every individual in the world has the kingdom of God within him and every individual has the Christ indwelling, it does not function except through his acknowledgment of it. It is not the truth that makes him free: it is his knowing of it that brings it into action.

## *You Carry Your Good with You*

To acknowledge that the kingdom of God is within you—the power, the dominion, and the presence of the indwelling Christ—is an important step in the direction of bringing about your own resurrection from the tomb of sin, of disease, poverty, unemployment, or the tomb of bad business. Another important step forward is to remind yourself daily of the truth of withinness, that all good is already within you, never to be achieved but only expressed.

When you enter an empty room there is no love there, neither is there any hate, sin, or disease. If a person went into a room to get anything, he would leave disappointed, for there is nothing in the room to be gotten. Whatever is in the room has to be brought there by the people who go into it. If there is love, it is because the people in it have brought love, and those who carry love into a room will walk out of the room with love multiplied. If anyone goes into a room with hate, envy, and jealousy, he will probably walk out with hate, envy, and jealousy multiplied.

An illustration of this, which occurred some years ago, was the case of a man who came to me for physical healing and explained that he had been to many practitioners and teachers and yet had not received his healing, although he attended church regularly and was faithful and loyal. It was just a flash of inspiration that led me to ask, "Why do you go to church?"

It took him some little time to solve that one, but finally he came up with an answer, "Oh, to learn more about God."

"You mean that after all these years that you've been attending church you haven't yet learned about God? You're still going there to learn about God?"

"Well no, not exactly. I know something about God, but if I learn more, I'll benefit more."

"And so the reason you go to church, then, is so that you will get some personal benefit?"

He had not thought about it in that way, and therefore he floundered because he could not explain his real reason for going to church. Thereupon, I pointed out to him that he would get out of church whatever he brought to it and added: "How about reversing your attitude and, the next time you go to church, go with the idea of taking something there with you? You already have some understanding of truth, of God, and of prayer. Why not go there with the little grain of truth that we will admit you have, and try to put that grain of truth to work for the benefit of those who are there and who do not yet know what the realization of God can do? Spend that entire hour with the idea that whatever you have gained of understanding you are going to share with those in that church."

The second week he came to me and announced noticeable improvement, and the third week was able to confirm a complete healing.

There is nothing in life to be gotten—not even God, nor an understanding of God. All that is, already is. And all that is, is already wherever you are. The kingdom of God cannot be brought to you even by Jesus Christ. He merely announced that the kingdom of God is not lo here, or lo there, but that the kingdom of God is already within you. Holy mountains or holy temples will not reveal God, and certainly there is even less hope of finding God in a man or in a book. God must be sought where God is—within you.

It is not your becoming more loving that makes love operate for you. It is the realization that the nature of

God is love and the kingdom of love is already established within you.

So it is that there is no such thing as love in an empty room, and nothing of hate, envy, or jealousy either. It is just a room, an empty room—nothing more. You go into it, and whatever takes place there depends on what you have brought with you. If you have brought love, then love is there; but if you brought hate, envy, jealousy, malice, criticism, or condemnation, that is what is there. You did not find it there: you brought it there.

Do not go anywhere for love, and do not go to anyone for love or for friendship: carry love and friendship with you. Do not go to anyone for forgiveness: carry forgiveness wherever you go. Do not go into this world expecting understanding: carry understanding to those you meet, and whatever you carry with you will be returned unto you.

### The Bread You Cast Upon the Waters Returns to You

"Cast thy bread upon the waters: for thou shalt find it after many days."[8] The law is that the bread that you cast will return unto you multiplied. If love is not being returned to you, that is not the bread that you are casting upon the waters. If understanding, forgiveness, abundance, and sharing have not come to you, it is because you have not cast that bread upon the water, and if you have not, it cannot return to you. All the bread on the water is earmarked, earmarked for return to the person who placed it there. Whatever the name or nature of the bread that is cast upon the water—the sweet bread of love and life, or the sour bread of envy, jealousy, malice, resentment, and persecution—that is the nature of the bread that returns. Life is like a checkbook, and the person who tries to draw out what he has not put in, sooner or later, is in trouble.

There is no love in this world, but there is love in you and in me. There is no hate in this world, but there may be hate in you and in me. If we send that love or that hate out into the world, it is there to multiply and return. I have traveled in practically every country of the globe during the past fifty-three years, and although I have met with much love, I have never yet met with hatred, resentment, or bigotry. I have never known any of these to be aimed at me, or to reach or touch me. I have spent many years in countries where bigotry and class distinction were rife, but I have never experienced or known these.

This is not because of any virtue on my part. I was born and brought up in New York City, and in such an environment a person grows up side by side with white, with black, and with yellow, with Jew and with Gentile, with Protestant and with Catholic, and usually he is not aware of any distinctions until he is too old to have it make any difference to him. It is a blessing to be born and brought up in a city like that and to be educated in the public schools where the boy or girl sitting next to you may be the child of very wealthy parents, and the one on the other side of you may live across the way on the wrong side of the tracks. Because of this circumstance in the formative years of my life, I grew up without any knowledge of bias or bigotry, and therefore in all my travels I have not experienced these, but have had returned to me only that which I have carried with me.

Since those early days and because of whatever measure of enlightenment has come to me, I know that wherever I travel I will meet what I carry with me. And so whether I have to go into a business office, a church edifice, or a customs station at the border, I carry with me the recognition of the indwelling Christ, the realization that every individual in his true identity is the child of God. When the Master taught, "Call no man your father upon the earth: for one is your Father, which is in heaven,"[9] he was not talking only to his particular followers in the Holy Land. He was talking to the world! There is but one Father—the heavenly Father.

Consciously carry with you, wherever you go, the realization:

*I have but one Father, and he is not only my Father but the Father of every person I meet, be he white or black, yellow or brown, Jew or Gentile, friend or enemy. Regardless of his background or present status, I know that we are brothers, for there is but one Father, and we are all children of that one Father. Whether anyone else knows it or not, I know it, and that makes everyone I meet of the household of God.*

When you carry that in your consciousness, it is felt by those you meet.

## The World Gives Back to You Your Attitude Toward It

You have all had the experience of knowing someone—a minister, a leader, a practitioner, or a teacher—whose very presence made you feel comforted and clean, made you feel engulfed by a wave of love. You recognized it because in the consciousness of that person there was love: he was living his Christianity; he was living his religion; he was living his godliness; and by being in his presence, the love expressed by him enveloped you.

Conversely, some of you have probably been in the presence of a person who has made your flesh creep. You could feel the hatred, the bigotry, the lust, or the sensuality that emanated from his thought, and you wanted to run away, to withdraw from it; you may have felt nervous or fidgety; and you may even have had the experience of wanting to run home and take a bath. It is as Emerson said, "What you are … thunders so that I cannot hear what you say." We are always expressing our inmost self even when we are trying to hide it. Mostly we hide it only from ourselves, but those who meet us know us, sometimes better than we know ourselves.

All of this is due to ignorance. If you are carrying out into this world any resentment, any hatred, jealousy, bias, or bigotry, you are doing it because of ignorance. You do not really know what you are doing. The Master was right when he said of those who crucified him, "Father, forgive them; for they know not what they do."[10] It is not sinfulness on your part if you carry fear out into the world: it is ignorance. You do not know what you are doing. When you do know, you can change that by knowing the truth:

*There is an indwelling Christ. The spirit of God is within me, and the spirit of God is in every individual I shall ever meet.*

Carry that out into the world, and the world will change its attitude toward you.

Try to understand that nothing can enter your experience except through your consciousness, not a thing. It is through your consciousness that you take in or give out either ignorance or wisdom.

You impart yourself to others. People will be drawn to you if they feel warmth, joy, spirituality, and good because in the presence of those qualities they are finding only the love of God flowing through.

You can carry that attitude out to the salesmen or the buyers you meet, to the customers you serve and to the salespeople who serve you. By carrying the realized presence of God to them, many a time they are healed, and you may send them home from their work more blessed than they have ever been.

You are always imparting yourself to others by your state of consciousness. This fact reveals the true nature of the Christian life. The Christian life is not a way of going to God for something; it is not a life of getting: it is a life of giving.

There is no way for God to reach this world except through consciousness; there must be a consciousness through which it comes. That is the secret of healing. You cannot receive spiritual healing from just anybody on the street. It takes someone who has developed his consciousness to the point of being a transparency through which God functions, and the greater the degree of that transparency, the greater healing work he can do.

Know the truth, the truth that all power is given unto you—God-power and God-dominion over all the sin, disease, lack, and limitations of the world. Know the truth that the indwelling Christ in you and in every individual in the world is the resurrecting and healing Christ and is everoperative, even without being told what to do, or to whom. Carry that realization with you in your association with other people, until more and more you are told, "I feel comforted when I talk with you," or, "A burden falls away when I am with you." Then you will know that you have entered the Christian life, and that great reservoir of "withinness" at the center of your being is flowing forth into expression as love, peace, and joy.

## INSTRUCTIONS TO A STUDENT

You are trying to heal *persons,* and it will not work. You are meditating to realize God, then peeking to see what God does about the error. In proportion as you attain spiritual awareness, you will find that harmony is, and that you do not have to try to establish it, but only to recognize that it is so. Spiritual consciousness does not heal: it sees through appearances to what actually is.

Healings rarely take place as we, or the patient, expect. What we would like is to have the pain stop instantly, the fever dissolve, and the lump disappear. If the patient is receptive, what actually occurs is that a change of consciousness takes place. There is less reliance on, and joy in external things and conditions, and a correspondingly greater love for, and understanding of, the invisible, and then outer harmony becomes evident.

If some patients do not respond outwardly, it is because they have not yielded inwardly. We do not change the appearance. Our realization of the Christ opens the consciousness, and that changes and purifies it. Then, and only then, does the outer appearance conform to the inner consciousness. In fact, the outer condition is the state of consciousness externalized. There can be no outer change until an inner awakening occurs.

All spiritual light comes only after darkness. Do I not indicate that over and over again? When we are happy in our health, supply, and relationships, there is no spiritual progress. As the material conditions or persons fail us, we are driven to the spirit. Just note how often you feel pleased because of apparent harmony, and you will see why you must be jarred out of merely human good.

## Across the Desk

It is a great joy to watch the unfolding of The Infinite Way, principally because the increased activity is an indication of the students' success in living and practicing the specific principles which constitute the message.

To understand the nature of God is the great secret. Once the student perceives that God is not like anything he may have believed him to be, and in proportion as the nature of God is revealed to him, an understanding of prayer and meditation comes quickly. Only through prayer and meditation is the activity of the presence of God made practical in our daily affairs. Above all things, to understand that there is not a giving or a withholding God, not a rewarding or a punishing God, is to find peace, quiet, and release from anxiety and fear.

Do not feel that you must eternally chase God: rather, be still and let God catch up to you. Let God find you as you let God's love flow through you to your neighbor and especially to your enemy-neighbor.

There is a Christ, and to "be still" brings the experience of divine grace because of this ever-present spirit of God in man. "Be still." There is no need to tell God, to instruct, or to plead with him. "Be still." The all-knowing already knows, and the stillness brings the fruitage of God's knowing; God is love, and that stillness brings the fruitage of God's love; God's grace is ever with us, and that stillness reveals the fruitage of God's grace.

## ❖ 6 ❖

# BRINGING GRACE
# INTO ACTIVE EXPRESSION

RIGHTLY UNDERSTOOD, LIVING the principles of The Infinite Way leads to a life by grace rather than by law.

In the eighth chapter of Romans, Paul tells us that a mortal being is not under the law of God, neither indeed can be, and that it is not possible for a mortal being to please God. Because the people of the earth are mortal, they still have sin, disease, death, man's inhumanity to man, slavery, and poverty in their midst. It may be hard to believe or understand, but a considerable proportion of the three billion people who live on this earth are in a state of progressive starvation and malnutrition. How can such conditions exist on earth after 2,000 years of Christianity, 2,500 years of Buddhism, and 2,500 years of Taoism? Is not the answer simple? Those who are not under the law of God are not fed or sustained by God. In no way do they receive God's grace.

The Master Christ Jesus said, "If a man abide not in me, he is cast forth as a branch, and is withered."[1] Attending church on Sunday morning or belonging to some religious body, even the most advanced metaphysical group, does not constitute abiding in the Word and letting the Word abide in us. Belonging to any kind of organization, and even believing in it, does nothing for us. Believing is, of course, a step—probably a first step—but believing that there is a North Pole does not lead one to it. There is still the arduous journey to be taken to reach it after we know that there is a North Pole. Entirely different from that kind of journey is the spiritual journey leading to the Father's house.

## *Mere Belief in God Is Not Enough*

Millions of people believe fervently in God. In fact there are few people in all this world suffering from sin, disease, death, lack, and limitation who would not proclaim their belief in God, but their belief does them very little good; it does not save them from these evils.

Is there anyone in this whole world who does not know that the oceans are filled with fish, the air with birds, and the earth with coal, oil, diamonds, and rubies? Is there anyone who does not know that the sun, moon, and stars travel in their orbits to such a degree of perfection that their positions can be charted years in advance and that they travel on schedule down to the split second? Can anyone, therefore, fail to recognize that there must be something of an invisible nature, of an infinite, eternal, and intelligent nature which is the cause, the maintaining and sustaining power of these effects? But something more than a belief in God is necessary, and that something more is the experience of God.

"But ye are not in the flesh, but in the Spirit, if so be that the Spirit of God dwell in you."[2] That is the essence of every spiritual or mystical teaching throughout all time. *"If so be the spirit of God dwell in you,"* if we keep the Word alive in our consciousness, if we dwell in the secret place of the most High, none of the evils of the earth will come nigh our dwelling place—and *dwell* means to *live*, not to vacation there, but to *live* there.

## *Recognition of a Divine Principle of Life*

We believe that there is a God because we can see all the effects of its presence and activity in the world, and we know that behind these effects must be a cause, the nature of which must be something intelligent, loving, infinite in power, eternal, and immortal.

But now there is the next step: to make contact with it, to bring that cause into expression in our life. The real function of The Infinite Way, therefore, is to reveal that there is a first cause and to take the next step of revealing that a contact with the cause must be made and maintained.

All those on the path leading to the experience of God will some day have to come to that place where they can look out upon this world with the realization that there is an infinite wisdom and intelligence that has provided the riches of this universe for its people. Such a realization will automatically lead to the conviction that whatever this cause is, whatever the law is, it operates by divine grace, and that means it operates for its own purpose and plan, and not because the earth or the people of the earth are worthy or deserving.

The nature of God is such that nothing anyone can do will deflect God from his eternal plan. God cannot be influenced to do more than he is already doing, nor is there any crime anyone can commit that will stop God or prevent him from doing what he is already doing. We can keep God out of our individual experience, but that will not prevent our neighbor from having the full and complete blessing of the grace of God. It is true that we either become beneficiaries of divine grace, or we prevent its flow and activity by virtue of the fact that we have accepted the human mind with its belief in two powers, good and evil. It is this that constitutes our humanhood, and that is the reason for the sin, disease, and death on earth, the poverty, lack, wars, and slavery.

## *The Man of Earth*

The human mind has accepted two powers, the power of good and the power of evil, and the man of earth lives out from that basis. You and I are that man of earth, and we all have had some good experiences and some bad ones, some healthy experiences and some sick ones, some rich and some poor. That is because the human mind, which is made up of the belief in good and evil, is in control, and we are a house divided against itself.

As mere human beings, many of us have been able to live threescore years and ten, twenty, and sometimes thirty, this by virtue of air, food, exercise, and some measure of mental stimulation. It is a life of getting up in the morning, working hard all day, and being so exhausted that we sleep all night so that we may build up enough strength to do the same thing over again the next day. But that is not really living: that is merely existing. It is a form of existence, however, that is so valued that many people will not yield it up, and they try to preserve it even if that life has to be spent in poverty, in jail, or in a hospital. To live is quite a different thing than to exist. To live, it is necessary to have contact with one's source, with that great causative principle which sent us into individual expression.

Each one of us has a different function and a different purpose here on earth. No one can do another's work. Each one has a reason for being born, but as the man of earth not one of us is fulfilling the mission that God created him to perform. As the man of earth, we go through life alone, but paradoxically unable to get along alone. We develop a dependency on other men and women; we feel the need for others to make our experience complete, some to employ us, some to provide companionship, instruction, and care. The result is that we begin a long process of catering to those who, we think, can do something for us and avoiding like the plague those who, we know, are going to look to us to do something for them. And so life really becomes a chase.

### The Man Whose Being Is in Christ

The man who has his being in Christ does not have to concern himself with "man, whose breath is in his nostrils."[3] He does not have to seek out those with influence and attempt to curry their favor by catering to them or fawning over them, nor does he have to fear anyone or run away from anyone. The man who has his being in Christ is rooted and grounded in God. He is God-created, God-maintained, God-sustained, God-fed, God-directed, and God-led. Not only does he have an infinite sufficiency that flows from within as it is needed, but there are always the twelve basketsful left over to share with those who have not yet attained the realization of their own Christ-being. The man of earth lives continually in that realm of the little self, lives unto himself, his family, and his associates, always reaching out for those people and things he believes are necessary to his experience.

The man who has his being in Christ lives in an inner realization. As he sits in his garden for meditation, he may see red ginger, oleander, papaya trees, a pine tree, or a cup of gold; and as he ponders those, he looks down to the earth and knows that they are all rooted and grounded in the same earth. The same earth that produces a lily in one corner produces ginger in another corner and plumeria in still another. The same sunshine, the same rain, and the same earth produce an infinite variety of good in his garden.

On another occasion, the man who has his being in Christ may ponder the ocean, all that is on the ocean and the things beneath the ocean and in the ocean. He observes how the creative principle operates, producing the great variety of fishes and rocks, sometimes even colored flowers and coral, how everything is provided for, how everything in the bosom of the sea finds its own whether it has to swim against the current or with the current. There is no lack or limitation in the sea, and this is evidence, too, of one principle creating fish and rocks, caves and flowers, time and tides—one principle creating, maintaining, and sustaining! And the sea just rests in the bosom of itself and lets this great presence and power permeate it and perform its functions.

The man who is anchored in Christ turns within and understands that he, too, draws upon an inexhaustible source that is the causative and creative principle of life.

*I rest in the bosom of the Father, in the assurance of his word. I am one with that which created me. I am maintained and sustained by this infinite presence and power operating as my intelligence, my love, my life, my health, my guidance and direction, and as my relationships with all others in the world. I need not look to anything external to me for I have within me meat that the world knows not of—an infinity of supply, so much that I can always share the twelve basketsful left over for which I will never have a need.*

As we ponder these truths, there is a lessening of fear. We cannot now be permanently engulfed in lack even though we may temporarily go through a period of limitation until we are firmly rooted and grounded in this awareness. The disease that racks the body does not plague us quite so much, and we do not react to it quite so much because now we know that as soon as we have attained this inner contact, as soon as the spirit of the Lord God consciously dwells in us, this disease too will yield. Whatever our personal prison may be, it will not seem quite so hard to bear because we know now that it is a temporary experience and that this with which we are united is even now fulfilling its function of bringing about our freedom.

### Illumination, an Individual Experience

The task before us is to make the transition from being that man of earth to becoming that man who has his being in Christ. There must come to the consciousness of each one of us an experience, an experience that no one else can have for us. It is true that while we are still in darkness, we can, of course, be helped by someone else's light. The tax collector and the fisherman who became Jesus' disciples were given a measure of illumination and partook of the grace of God by virtue of their contact with the Master. Nevertheless he assured them that they of themselves would have to come to this experience in order for it to become permanent. "It is expedient for you that I go away: for if I go not away, the Comforter will not come unto you."[4]

Knowing the truth is the foundation and the connecting link which forms the basis of our life's demonstration. Unfortunately, there are too many students who think that their problems will be solved if they read enough inspirational statements in books or if they read a certain number of pages each day, and I think that some of our students now are beginning to feel that if they just hear enough recordings that that in and of itself will solve their problems. It is not true. There is no denying that those students who read The Infinite Way writings, listen to the recordings, and attend classes do benefit. They do have their lives changed for them, sometimes miraculously, and it is because of what it has done for those who have come to this work that The Infinite Way has gone around the world as it has in but sixteen years. I must warn our students over and over again, however, that in order to make this experience of harmony permanent and as infinite as it should and can be, they themselves must have this realization. Nothing can ever replace individual realization of truth.

Each one must and will, eventually, come to the experience of illumination. There is no time set. There is no need for hurry. There is an eternity in which to work out of the dullness and darkness of human sense, and in which to receive illumination from those who have already attained it and are always willing to share their light with their disciples, students, and followers.

Whether the experience comes with or without the guidance of one already illumined, it cannot occur except through an activity of our consciousness. Our life-demonstration will be only in proportion to the truth that we ourselves know, ponder, and meditate upon until it becomes our own experience of illumination. There is no such thing as vicarious spiritual attainment. It is something each one achieves through the activity of his own consciousness, and it is attained in proportion to his degree of devotion, not only to study but to putting into practice what has been studied.

"The kingdom of God is within you,"[5] but it is necessary to sit in quietness and to be at peace to make this contact with that kingdom, so that in addition to what we read or hear we begin to receive impartations from within. When we begin to receive impartations, we have made at least a start on the spiritual path.

## The Sacredness of a
## Spiritual Experience Compels Secrecy

It is at this point that we must be most careful because it is then that we need not only the realization that this is a sacred experience, but also that it is a secret one. To expect anyone to believe what unfolds from within would be like trying to tell a blind man about the beauties of an orchid. He has no way of visualizing what the orchid is like, nor does the man of earth have any way of knowing what manner of life is lived by the man who has his being in Christ. Never should these things be spoken of indiscriminately because our "pearls" will be trampled upon, and even our faith may be taken away from us. It is so easy for a person to say that a really deep and significant spiritual experience could not, and did not, happen, that it was just a meaningless dream and that we were imagining things, until his skepticism causes doubt to creep in and rob us of our joy.

These experiences on the spiritual path are sacred, and not only do not come to anyone except through an intense devotion that makes for sacredness, but they will not abide unless they are kept secret. It is true that there are some friends with whom we can share these things, but they are friends who have had the same experiences. We need never hesitate to share our experiences with the illumined, however, because they know the language we are speaking. They know what these experiences mean, and in some measure they themselves have had them, if not exactly the same ones or in the same way, at least they have had enough to know that what we are sharing is a precious "pearl."

*Resting in the Invisible*

Through meditating and pondering truth, a time comes when the "click" takes place within, a definite awareness that something has happened that never happened before, and from then on we nurse it. We retire into ourselves more and more frequently, not for long periods of time, but many times a day and several times a night until we are so well established in God that there does not even seem to be a human selfhood left to care for. This other thing is caring for us. It provides in advance for something of which we have no knowledge of needing at the present time. There is an invisible wisdom governing our life; there is an invisible love enfolding us, providing, caring, protecting, and sustaining.

It is through our own dedication and consecration that we bring this about. It will not happen to us "out of the blue," although it has happened occasionally to a few persons who, without even having a thought in their mind of a spiritual subject, suddenly have had an experience such as this, but then because they knew nothing of its nature very often they have lost it and have been unable to recapture it. That is not true of us because when we have the experience, we know why we have it. We know that the divine presence, the Holy Ghost, has descended upon us; and we know that since this is true, we can return again and again and again to this quiet withinness and bring it back into conscious expression until eventually the day comes when this is no longer necessary, and the Christ is really living our life. The ultimate is being reached, and then we become so established in this that there really is no little "I" to take care of. Something invisible is always doing the taking care of in advance.

*All that the Father, the invisible infinite, has is made manifest through my individual being. This inner meat that I have, and which the world knows nothing of, appears outwardly as food on my table. This spiritual water that I have within bubbles up into life eternal. This power of divine grace that is now mine by virtue of my oneness with God becomes my resurrection, and even my body is raised up out of the tomb of disease, the tomb of old age, or the tomb of infirmity and is restored again to its normalcy and harmony.*

*As I consciously realize that I am fed from within, and that all that the Father has is flowing in me and through me, even the lost years of the locust are restored: the money that has been lost or dissipated begins to return, reputations that have been ruined are remade, and the body that was weak and ailing is restored to health.*

*Out of this infinity, all things become new. All that I shall ever need is given to me from the infinite source within my being, continuously fulfilling God's plan as individual being.*

### Bringing Our Lives into Conformity<br>To the Pattern Shown Us on the Mount

It is possible for every person in the entire world to experience this joy, but each one has to come to it individually. No one can do it for anyone else. The whole distance must be traveled by the individual.

There are those who can be a help to us, who can shorten the time and relieve us of many of the human burdens of our experience, but let us always remember that these are temporary dispensations. The final attainment is the one we, ourselves, achieve through a conscious activity of our consciousness.

We must know the truth *consciously*. We must do our own meditating. Whether it is contemplating the mysteries of a garden, the illimitability of the ocean, or the grandeur of an unscalable mountain, we must find something to take into our meditation that we can ponder, something that will bring us eventually to the realization of this that underlies the visible and which permeates it, creating, animating, maintaining, and sustaining.

"Thou will keep him in perfect peace, whose mind is stayed on thee.[6] ... In quietness and in confidence shall be your strength."[7]

*I will meditate upon the Lord all the day and all the night. I will meditate upon the Lord. "I will lift up mine eyes unto the hills, from whence cometh my help."[8] I will live and move and have my being in divine consciousness. I will dwell in the Word, and let the Word dwell in me.*

All this must become a part of our consciousness, but in addition to that we have the obligation of adhering to the pattern given us by the Master by which we mold our lives in order to maintain the spiritual life. First of all, we must pray for forgiveness of our own sins. There is no one on this earth so righteous that he is not daily sinning against the Holy Ghost. Every time that we bear false witness against a neighbor, every time we indulge our hate, fear, jealousy, animosity, bigotry, or bias, we are sinning. Sins are not just those major offenses against society and individuals that most people have overcome before they enter the spiritual life, but sin is something that normally we do not even consider as sin. It is necessary, therefore, that we pray frequently and seriously to be forgiven those sins of omission and commission that may be soiling us and keeping us from being a transparency, those bits of darkness that accumulate and withhold the light.

The second step is to engage in these periods of forgiveness for the dictators of the world, and especially for those who would personally harm us—persecute, lie, or cheat—realizing that it is but the carnal mind and that it exists only as the "arm of flesh" and is without power. Let us make sure that we are living in an atmosphere of continuous love and forgiveness, and even though we may thoughtlessly indulge at times in resentment or animosity, let us retire quickly into the silence and begin a period of self-forgiveness as well as forgiveness of all others.

Life was not meant for the glorification of ourselves. We do not have the right to seek things for our self or for our personal glory. We must show forth the glory of God in service to man. We cannot live unto ourselves, or for ourselves. The wonderful things of life that are given to us—and they do come bountifully, abundantly, joyously—come not for us, but that God's grace may be witnessed and may be used for the benefit of mankind.

No great spiritual leader from the earliest days to the most modern of metaphysical days has ever lived unto himself or for himself. His life has always been a continual giving of himself and his possessions to the work and to those who partake of that work. So it is that we never receive anything of God that *we* may be glorified, or that *we* may be enriched, or that *we* may be healed. Everything that we receive, we receive in order to bear witness to God's goodness and God's presence and God's grace.

## Instructions to a Student

We must instantly recognize appearances of every name and nature as being the carnal mind appearing as form. These forms may appear as persons, conditions, or circumstances, but our work is the instantaneous recognition of the truth that, regardless of the form, the substance is the carnal mind, or the universal belief in two powers.

When we accept any form or appearance as something of itself, as something separate and apart from the carnal mind, we are in the dream; but if we instantly recognize all appearances as the carnal mind appearing as form, and understand, of course, that the carnal mind is but a universal belief in two powers and is therefore not God-ordained, has no substance, no law, and cannot be cause or effect, we have then overcome the world.

To transcend the dream, then, really means the instantaneous recognition of all appearances as substanceless carnal mind.

## Across the Desk

Life is not a bargain for those who live merely from morning to night, or even live from day to day. Life is an experience only when we break through the parenthesis of human existence and taste of immortality here and now. Life cannot be a joy to those who cater only to the mortal side of humanity: it becomes a delight only when we can commune with the Soul of men and women, commune with one another in spiritual association. Only the sensualist finds satisfaction in seeing the outward form of persons, but heaven itself is revealed as we see the Soul and commune with the spirit, the reality, of one another.

Limitation exists only in the dream of life, not in life itself. Fear exists only in the dream of two powers, not in omnipotence. Disease exists only in the dream of mortality, not in the immortal being which you are and which I am.

We break the parenthesis of human life to circle eternity. We break the bonds of limitation to experience the infinity of his grace. We break the fetters of mortality to clothe ourselves with immortality.

## ❖ 7 ❖

# THE POWER TO BECOME
# THE SON OF GOD

LIFE IS A MATTER of individual demonstration. Hundreds of persons may be exposed to the same truth, but only a few will benefit from it. The words each person reads may be the same, and the consciousness back of those words the same, but the difference lies in individual receptivity and individual responsiveness to the spiritual word. The benefit derived by any person results by virtue of some active receptivity within him.

Those of you who have had experience in the healing work must realize this. If ten patients come into your orbit in a single day and you give the same degree of integrity to each one, the same understanding, consciousness, and faithfulness in treatment, one of them may receive an instantaneous healing; three, very quick healing; three, long drawn out and protracted healing; and others, no healing. Why is that? In every case, the treatment was equally able and faithful, so what is the difference?

The difference is in the degree of spiritual receptivity in the consciousness of the person who is seeking your help. He may have it in great or slight degree, or he may have no spiritual receptivity whatsoever. That is no reason for criticism or praise because no one is responsible for the degree of his receptivity or spiritual integrity. That is a matter over which he has no control. Some people have come into this world more spiritually blessed and more spiritually receptive than others, whereas some have come into this world more materialistically inclined, and they, therefore, will have a greater struggle developing the necessary spiritual receptivity and responsiveness.

When a practitioner begins to work with a patient or student, it is not possible to know whether he will have an instantaneous or a slow healing because the practitioner does not know the factors that are involved. He does not know what there is in the patient's consciousness that may be blocking the message or preventing the spiritual activity from breaking through. Some patients are so intent on getting well if they have been sick, or on attaining abundance and security if they have been suffering from lack that it is difficult for them to center their attention on the most important factor, awareness of God.

In seeking the conscious realization of God's presence, all things are added—peace, harmony, joy, health, and prosperity—but they are the added things that come after some measure of realization of God has been attained. It is the responsibility of the practitioner or teacher to lead the student away from whatever it is he is trying to attain and to help him to break the pattern of seeking persons and things, safety and security, peace and joy, by turning his attention to seeking the kingdom of God so that he may experience the joy of feeling the presence of God within him.

## Zeal Is Not Enough

Too often, after they have gained a smattering of truth, students in their zeal and enthusiasm rush out to try to save the world, little realizing that acquiring a firm foundation in the letter of truth is essential as a first step before any work with others can be attempted. Students are often shocked when I tell some of them that they have no right to preach truth to anyone; they have no right to proselyte or to try to save the world: they are not equipped or ready for it. They are trying to give truth to the world before they themselves have anything to give. They have zeal, but not understanding or wisdom, and do not realize that before they can benefit the world, they must have contact with God; they must achieve a conscious realization of the presence of the Father within.

It is not enough, however, merely to know the letter of truth, to know that the books say that God is within. It is not enough to prate, "Oh, error isn't real." Certainly knowledge of the letter of truth is requisite as a foundation on which to take the next step of conscious realization of the presence of God, but *knowledge* alone is not sufficient for one to go out into the world trying to give to the world what these students themselves often do not have. No one should go out voicing truth, preaching, proselyting, and trying to save other persons until he has been called.

Only when you have come to a place in consciousness where you consciously tabernacle with God, and can sit quietly and peacefully until you feel God's presence, are you ready to go out into the world because then you have that and only that which will save the world—God. Knowledge about God will not do it: only one thing will do it—God itself.

## *The Word That Is with Power*

If you have had any experience in the healing work, you must realize that there is no use searching around in your mind for some powerful or deep truth because it is not going to help either you or your patient. Only one thing is going to be of any help—God. Your knowledge of truth will lift you and bring you into an atmosphere of consciousness in which God can be felt, realized, and attained, but that is as far as any truth you know will take you.

The statements of truth that you may make in an attempt to help yourself or someone else are worthless, but if you will declare whatever truth you know and open your consciousness for truth to flow into you until the "click" comes which assures you of the presence of God, then you will find that the statements you voice are the word of God which is quick and sharp and powerful. Statements of truth made out of the mind are not the word of God. If they were, they would not return unto you void, and all treatments would be more fruitful.

Begin your treatment work with whatever statements or quotations of truth you can remember. Then, let truth reveal itself within until you feel the "click." From that moment on, the real treatment begins, because whatever word of truth comes through when you are in spiritual consciousness will prove to be the word of God.

From that height of spiritual enlightenment, in an exalted state of consciousness, dwelling in God, you can speak truth to anyone because you are speaking to the individual's Christhood. If you are consciously one with God, you are consciously one with your patient; then, in communion with the Soul of his inner being, the words come: What did hinder you? Rise, take up your bed, and walk. You are pure spirit. There is no power hindering you from fulfilling your spiritual destiny. You are the very Soul which is God, God-life itself. You are pure, God itself in expression. You were never born, and you will never die. You have no need of demonstrations—physical, mental, moral, or financial—because in reality you are in heaven now.

Such words are not your words, but the word of God: you are living in the consciousness which is the kingdom of God, and it is revealing the person's inner integrity, his inner being and Soul. You are not addressing Jim, Bill, or Mary, or any other person by name: you are speaking directly to the Soul, but from your own Soul, and not from your mind or from something that you have read in a book. It is the very Soul of God pouring itself through you into the Soul of the individual to whom you are speaking.

Never forget that there is no truth you will ever read anywhere that is true about a human being. It is not correct to say that a human being is spiritual, perfect, or the child of God. A human being, a mortal, is on his way to death. Human beings were born, are maturing, aging, and will die. To talk about them as though they were spiritual and children of God is utter nonsense. It is no wonder that the world ridicules and scoffs at metaphysicians for walking around saying, "Error isn't real," while it is biting their heels; or, "I am joint-heir with Christ in God, but I don't know where my next month's rent is coming from." A human being is not a child of God; a human being is not spiritual; a human being is not on his way to heaven; a human being has no spiritual hope.

However, when you have had sufficient meditation to lift yourself to that point where you receive the "click," you can speak right into the Soul of any person, "You are the beloved of God." As a human being he is not; but as a spiritual being he is. When you have lifted yourself into that mind that was in Christ Jesus, you can also say, "Rise, and walk."

If you will remember that the object of The Infinite Way is to overcome material sense and be lifted into spiritual consciousness, you will have very little difficulty in healing work. The difficulty arises when somebody has a fever and you try to reduce it: that is a very hard thing to do, sometimes impossible. When somebody has a lump and you want to help him get rid of it, or when someone is unemployed and you attempt to help him obtain employment, or when someone is in lack and you want to demonstrate abundance, your practice becomes heavy and hard. If, on the other hand, you will relinquish all desires in that direction and devote yourself to attaining the conscious realization of God's presence, harmony will appear in the experience of those who turn to you for help.

## *All Truth Is Embodied in the Word* I

Healing work in The Infinite Way does not concern itself with people: it concerns itself with principles of life. The most basic of these principles is found in the word I. The I has no reference to Jim, Bill, or Mary: the word I means God. Therefore, God being I, God constitutes your being and mine; God is your individual Soul and mine. It is like the electric light fixtures in your home. There is only one electricity, but each of these fixtures is receiving and using the same electricity. So, too, there is only one God, one Soul, but each one in his spiritual identity is constituted of that one Soul, one life, one God.

And what is the nature of that God? In Scripture, it is said that God is a power, and since the command is to have only one God, it must mean that you must have only one power. Not only is there but one power, but the I of you is that power. It is not a power that operates on you; it is not a power that operates in you; it is not a power that operates through you. The I of your own being is that power, and it is infinitely good. It never has to be used to overcome error, to heal disease, or to create supply.

In the world of appearances are sin, disease, lack, and limitation, but you are not dealing with the world of appearances: you are dealing with principles that must be brought to your conscious remembrance when you sit down for the purpose of benefitting yourself or others. You are going to God, you are going into the depth of your consciousness, retiring into the inner sanctuary, and there you tabernacle with truth, and the truth is I. I constitutes your individual being and mine, and that I is the only power; therefore, there is no need for it to be used against sin, disease, or death. It must be recognized, acknowledged, and eventually it must be realized. I, I in the midst of you is the only power. Rest in that truth. Do not go any further; rest in it. That is enough. I, the I of you is God, and the I of you is power, and there are no other powers.

As you go further in Scripture, you will learn that God is law. And what is God? I! Then I is law. Then I, the I of your own being, is law, and since you are to have no other God but one, you can have no law but one. Are there material laws? Are there mental laws? Are there financial laws? Are there governmental laws? No, there is only one law, and the I of you is that law. Rest in that:

*God is the* I *of my being, and that* I *is the only power, the only presence, and the only law.*

*"Hear, O Israel: The Lord our God is one Lord"* [1]—*just one, one, one. Therefore,* I *am that one.*

I is that one whether that I is Jim, Bill, or Mary, but never speak this of a human being and claim divinity for him. This would be a sin, a sin against the Holy Ghost. Only in the depths of your sacred and secret being dare you accept the truth that the I of you is God, the I of me is God, and the I of the worm or the mosquito is God. In fact, all the life of this world is embodied in this I, all the truth, all the love.

As you ponder and dwell on that, it fills your consciousness. What you are entertaining in your consciousness becomes evident. You need not speak of it to anyone you meet. If you are leading a life dedicated to the study of spiritual wisdom and if you are keeping your thought centered on spiritual things, there is something in your face that reveals it; whereas if you are busy pursuing the pleasures of this world, this, too, is revealed in your face.

And so it is that the truth you are entertaining in your consciousness is producing healing for the world that touches you, without your ever voicing one word of truth to the people of that world. Outside of my work with students, I seldom voice truth. Those receptive and responsive to the spiritual impulse will be blessed by any person who maintains truth in his consciousness, and he need not voice it, although when a direct question is asked the right answer is given, and the right answer is never, "I am God," or "I am spirit," or "I am spiritual," or "I am a child of God." Those are statements never to be made to the profane thought.

### God Is Not Separate and Apart from You

When you are in meditation, contemplating God and the things of God, it is important to know that God is not something separate and apart from you, nor is there a law of God, or a presence or a power of God separate and apart from you. The very *I* of your being is God.

It is for that reason that you have no demonstration of health, wealth, safety, or security to make. How can God have need of those things? How can *I* have need of those things? *I am. I* already am. *I* am that *I AM. I* am He that should come. Those things are to be taken into secret meditation and realized about your own inner true being and about the inner true being of all mankind, whether friend or foe.

You are not dealing with appearances: you are dealing with principles; and it makes no difference whether you are talking about Jew or Gentile, white or black, Occidental or Oriental. The same truth is true—*I, I, I:*

*Where I am, God is. The whole presence and power of God is in the* I *that* I *am. If I ride in a plane,* I *do not: the plane rides in me. And if I go down in a submarine,* I *do not: the submarine rides in me. I live and move and have my being in* I.

If you were to take the mental approach to life and try to demonstrate something, it would have to be based on the premise that you are a human being, and probably one who is in lack, limitation, sin, or disease; and even if you should derive some benefit from that, in the end you would be just a human being who is better off than he was before. You still would not have touched your spiritual identity or made way for the kingdom of heaven to be established in you. If, on the other hand, you begin with the basic principle *I,* that God is *I,* that God is the *I* of your being, and that this *I* which you are embodies all the presence and power of the Godhead, and then realize that since God is one, there is but one presence and one power, you will have no fighting to do, and no overcoming.

The overcoming is in the human being overcoming being a human being, which Paul calls "dying daily." But you "die daily" only in proportion as you starve out your human selfhood and let it "die." You let it die by consciously abiding in the word *I* and in the fact that that *I* is the only One.

Since there is only one power, you are under no necessity of protecting yourself from any evil power. That *I*, being the infinite One, you have no need of safety or security, and you have no need of peace, you have no need of anything.

That *I* is Self-created, Self-maintained, Self-sustained. Therefore, it never looks outside of itself for anything. You may be thankful to parents who have left you a large inheritance; you may be grateful to an employer who pays you well; you may appreciate your husband or wife who provides for you. You may do that, but you have no right to be dependent on any one of them, or to feel that some person is the source of your good. True, you not only may, but you must, be grateful to others for everything that you receive from them, but at the same time you must never forget the source.

Another basic point is implied in this *I:* What you accept for yourself, you must accept for every other person because there is only one *I.* So if someone says that he is ill, and you know that you are not, you do not have to accept that and you do not have to reject it. On the other hand, if you accept the fact that the *I* of you is God, then you do not have to pay any attention at all to what anyone may say because God is the *I* of you. If you learn to accept everyone in your consciousness as God-being, you need have no fear for him. If, however, you accept him as a human being, then you will have concern.

*I* is the beginning of your meditation work. What you find to be true of *I* will appear outwardly as the truth about Jim, Bill, or Mary. So do not concern yourself with knowing the truth about a person: know the truth about *I.* Then, as you realize *I* to be true identity and that true identity being one, you have only one power to deal with—one presence, one law, one cause—and *I* is that.

## *Placing Power in Form or Effect Is the Error*

All error is made up of the belief that there is power in certain forms or effects. For example, if you believe that life is dependent on the heart, you are giving power to a form; therefore it becomes necessary specifically to know that life is not dependent on organs and functions, for life is God and is Self-maintained and Self-sustained. There is, also, a universal belief in the power of germs, in some germs an evil, deadly power and in some germs a good and healing power. Such belief is erroneous because it places power in form, in an effect called a germ, and there is no power in form or effect: all power is in the invisible.

The error is not the germ, not the weather, and not the climate: the error is in the belief that these have power. Do not deny weather; do not deny climate; do not deny infection or contagion; do not deny horoscopes; but realize that because there is only one power, there is no power in form or in effect. Then you will be handling error.

Error is a belief that there is power outside of God, outside of the *I* that you are. It is in the belief that the heart, the lungs, or some other organ of the body can do something, or be something, whereas it cannot do or be anything but an instrument for *I*. Whether it is an instrument for good or for evil depends on to what extent you are operating on the spiritual or the human plane.

The moment that you surrender yourself to the government of the *I* which is God, every organ of your body is then not your instrument, but the instrument of God. It has no power to live or to die; it has no power to give or to withhold: it has only the power to be an instrument through which God works.

The human being can be good or he can be evil; he can do good or he can do evil; he can be sick or well; and he can be alive or dead—if he is operating from the standpoint of being man, that is, of being effect. The moment that you make the transition and realize, "No, I is God. 'I live; yet not I, but Christ liveth my life,'"[2] the body becomes an instrument through which God lives. Then the body cannot be sick, and it cannot be well; it cannot be alive or dead: the body can only be an instrument through which God functions.

In your earliest stage on the spiritual path, you may occasionally forget that your body is but an instrument through which God functions, and instead of being the master of it, you may let universal belief operate upon it. Experiences that come as a result of the operation of universal belief are just lessons along the way and provide opportunities to expand consciousness. No one can jump into heaven at a single bound, so if you fall down once in a while, do not criticize or condemn yourself. Give yourself a little time to assimilate the idea that this is not your body: this is the body of God, the temple of the Holy Ghost, and it is God's responsibility to operate it, not yours.

Error consists in placing power in person, thing, circumstance, or condition. Regardless of what problem your patient presents to you, it usually takes the form of some power that he gives to somebody or something. You must realize that that is the error, that it is not power and not place, not cause, and that it does not have an effect.

All the power and all the glory and all the dominion are in the I that you are. It is an easy thing to state that God is all and that there is no error: it is a difficult thing to demonstrate. It becomes simpler if, when you are called upon to help others, you ask yourself, "To what am I giving power? Germs, infection, heredity, horoscopes, the calendar, age?"

There is the error: the belief in a selfhood apart from God, a presence and a power apart from God, and the belief that there is a God other than the I which you are. Everyone that experiences any discord at all is being handled by a universal belief, some universal error.

As long as you are in this flesh, it will be necessary to bring to your conscious remembrance the truth that the I is God, not man, not effect, I is spirit, and that I embodies within itself all presence, all power, all law, all cause, and all effect. From there, go on to the realization that whatever it is that is troubling you is a belief in a power external to your own being, a power in effect, in form, or in person.

The Master had to meet the belief in a power external to himself when he came face to face with Pilate. So, in facing infection, contagion, temptation, unhappiness, loneliness, lack, and limitation, you have to know that there is no power in them: the power is in the God that is the *I* of you—the power of the *I-am-ness* within you.

No statement of truth is power unless it is uttered when you are in the spirit. "If so be that the spirit of God dwell in you,"[3] then are you the children of God—then are you the Christ, the Savior, then are you the son of God that has power to forgive sin, heal disease, and raise the dead. If you are not in the spirit, you are just a human being trying to take unto yourself powers that you never have had, and never will have. It is only the son of God in you that has power. Not by man or by ordination of man, not by licensing by man, not by receiving an authority from man or organization does a man become an apostle. That which constitutes Christhood is an inner ordination from God which is the spirit of God in man. You and I as human beings have to lift ourselves into the attainment of that divine Son-ship, and then do we receive power to become sons of God.

## Across the Desk

Occasionally, in a new seeker, I find a sense of futility with life in general, a feeling of "what is the use," almost a giving up. Always my answer is that this is perfectly natural to an individual who no longer loves, gives, and shares. Seldom do we find futility in those who love and serve. The givingness of life comes forth from the lovingness of the Soul, and this makes life an adventure and a joy. Not who loves us or how many love us, not who gives to us or shares with us, but whom do we love, to whom do we minister, with whom do we share: this is the secret of a life of joy and peace.

Those of us who commune with the stars and the sea or the mountains will understand the love that wells up as they reveal their mysteries to us. There is mystery in the calm sea and in the boisterous waves; there is a miracle in the stars; and when stars and sea talk to us, the ecstasy of life fills soul and mind and body. Those who know that there is more to a dog, a horse, or a cat than meets the eye also find that same mystery unveiled in the communion that takes place between a man and a beloved pet.

Who can read of enslaved peoples or pauperized natives without pouring out love to those not yet awakened, and coming more alive in the love we pour out? We live again in the love we give to them.

Resurrection? Perhaps you have not believed in resurrection. Give yourself, give your help to those who are now what your ancestors and mine were as they came to these shores destitute—political, religious, or economic slaves—and witness your own resurrection, and you will believe in it. Will we live again? Find someone or something to love, and find a new life, your eternal life. When love is gone from one, futility sets in. When love steals in, life begins again.

# ✢ 8 ✢

# RISING ABOVE "THIS WORLD"

AS HUMAN BEINGS, WE are made up of theories and beliefs—false education, false religious knowledge, and superstition. For example, there are few persons in all this land who do not believe that God punishes and God rewards, and furthermore that God will destroy all their enemies and discords if, through some kind of hocus-pocus or abracadabra, they can get on the right side of God.

It is difficult to empty out the old bottles and free ourselves from the concepts to which we have clung throughout the years. It is not easy to develop a flexibility which permits the old forms to be broken up, making way for the new wine of the spirit. Every time we are faced with some absolute spiritual truth, we unconsciously reject it and then experience repercussions because of the inner conflict that is set up. We are continually looking back and comparing this new truth with what we have heretofore believed and which is so firmly rooted in us that it really goes beyond belief to absolute conviction. In fact, we would sacrifice almost anything in the world before we would give up our cherished beliefs.

"The Wisdoms of The Infinite Way"[1] contain some of this new wine that will help sweep aside old concepts. Every one of these "Wisdoms" came through revelation, most of them by my being awakened in the middle of the night and having to get up and write down the particular "Wisdom" that revealed itself. All told, they comprise only a few pages, and yet the contents of those few pages were two years in being unfolded to me. The study of these wisdoms can carry the student into a whole new realm of consciousness as it has already done with some of the few students who were given these wisdoms for study and meditation long before they were released to the public in an additional chapter in *The Infinite Way.*

### All Illusion Is a Mental Image in Thought

From birth, we are faced with appearances which are the source of all the troubles that befall us. To realize the nonpower of these appearances that are a constant source of discord and inharmony in our life, requires an understanding of the nature of error, a subject that many people do not enjoy dwelling upon.

As a matter of fact, however, the correct understanding of the nature of error can become our salvation because this makes it possible to understand the allness of God, whereas studying the allness of God unrelated to the nature of error would never enable us to grasp God's allness.

There is, perhaps, not a single religion in the world that does not acknowledge God as the only power, and because of this very acknowledgment the terrible afflictions which people suffer are attributed to the inscrutable will of God, thus making God responsible for all the tragedies on earth: storms at sea, hurricanes, volcanoes, and man's inhumanity to man.

If we judge by appearances, we certainly must admit that there are sick, sinful, and dying people; there are accidents and all manner of disasters and man-made catastrophes. But because we acknowledge God as the only power, are we to lay the responsibility for the errors of the world at the door of God? And yet there is no other way out of that dilemma, nor is there any escape from it if we continue to judge by appearances.

There have been spiritually illumined persons on earth who have realized that there is no death, and some who have even seen that there is no birth, and still others who have recognized that there is no disease on earth and no reality to any negative appearance. The revelation that came to Gautama the Buddha under the Bodhi tree was that all appearance is illusion; it is not reality and is not taking place in time or space: it is taking place only in a universal mortal concept of the universe.

That was Jesus' vision when he looked at Pilate and said, "Thou couldest have no power,"[2] although all appearances testified to the fact that Pilate was the ruler of the land and had all power. Jesus was able also, to see disease in its severest forms and say, "Rise, take up thy bed, and walk."[3] He was able to look at sin and dismiss it with a "Neither do I condemn thee,"[4] not condoning it, but recognizing that sin, as sin, does not exist.

Very little of that principle was understood in the years following Jesus, although during that time there were some deep mystics, men who had attained conscious union with God, and yet in their conscious oneness with God, they did not perceive that making God responsible for the errors of the world simply intensified their reality. Not until the advent of modern metaphysics was it made clear again that God is the only power and that these appearances of discord do not have reality. In the early years whenever troubles were brought to the practitioner of modern metaphysics, he could smile and turn away without reacting to them—without fearing them and without protecting himself from them—merely by perceiving that whatever it is that appears as an evil person or condition can be instantly dismissed as nothingness.

But just as the teaching of the illusory nature of error was lost after the generation of Gautama the Buddha, so has it been all but lost in present-day metaphysics. Those not close to Gautama accepted the teaching that sin, disease, and death were illusions, but they believed that these illusions were externalized as form, and therefore they looked upon them as something to be destroyed. So today diphtheria, influenza, or any other disease is considered by many metaphysicians to be an illusion, but an illusion to be removed.

Originally, the meaning of the teaching of the illusory origin of disease was that, even though it was called diphtheria or influenza, it was only a mental image or nothingness. An illusion or a mental image in thought has no substance or reality: it is merely an unfounded belief about something, a rumor. And yet how many students of metaphysics who have left behind them the habit of saying, "I have a cold, the flu, or the grippe," will call and ask for help explaining that they have an illusion, and then in the next breath add, "Will you help me get rid of it? Will you do some protective work to save me from the illusion?"

This misinterpretation of a really deep spiritual teaching goes back to innate human nature which has accepted and lives by two powers: the power of good and the power of evil. Always the human being is swinging back and forth between the pairs of opposites instead of seeing the infinite and eternal allness of the spiritual universe and knowing all error to be nothingness, illusion, a false sense of something.

## *Fear of Extinction, the Basic Error*

There are no powers of evil external to yourself. Discords have no external existence. Resolve them within your own consciousness.[5]

When we begin to understand the nature of error as an appearance that has no concrete existence, no outlined form, and that it is not an externalized physical condition, but a mental image in thought, existing nowhere except in our limited vision of that which is, we no longer battle sin, disease, death, lack, or limitation, and through this realization we arrive at a conviction of God's allness. Eventually, this understanding leads to the ultimate realization of the reasons why there is error anywhere on earth, why it ever appeared on earth, and what it is that perpetuates it.

There is only one error on all the earth and that is the fear of extinction, the fear of the loss of the little "I" that would rather be on this earth eighty years than sixty, or the little "I" that is in prison, fighting and sometimes spending a fortune to avoid the death penalty only in order to remain in a prison for the rest of his life. Even though a person knows that such living is going to be worse than death, at least he has the certainty that it will be some form of "I," even though that "I" continues to walk around in a dungeon.

We all want to preserve this sense of "I," even in its miseries. We cling to a sense of "I": it is that "I" that we want made and kept comfortable; it is that I that we would like to glorify by having ourselves placed in some position of authority or by achieving fame and seeing our name in print.

This false sense of "I" comes as a temptation to the neophyte on the spiritual path, but it is an even greater temptation to those who have achieved some measure of success in the spiritual ministry. Then the ego may attempt to vaunt itself and even lead the unwary so far astray as to cause him to boast about his spiritual attainments or to be so unethical as to divulge confidences by talking about specific cases of healing in which he has been instrumental. The ego is continually talking in terms of "I," "me," or "mine": "I did this," or "I did that"; "my" this, that, or the other thing; and by its much calling attention to itself tries to bolster its illusion of self or hide its own emptiness and nothingness, forgetting:

> There is no such thing as "my harmony," "my health," or "my supply." *His peace* passeth all understanding. *His grace* is sufficient.
> Withdraw from personal consciousness as rapidly as possible. Let "I" die.[6]

As long as there is a false sense of I to which we cater and which we worship and feed, there will be fear for it, and that will lead to every error on earth. The basic factor is fear of the extinction of the personal sense of I. For example, there is the fear that some unimportant incidence of disease can grow to such proportions that it will kill us. The only reason that we fear unemployment is that we may starve or freeze to death. No matter how mild the form of sickness may be, there is always the fear that it may lead to death. Entertaining the false sense of I sets up fear, and it is fear not only of ultimate extinction, but also of temporary discomfort. On the other hand, in proportion to our loss of fear, the errors themselves disappear.

## *Losing the False Sense of "I"*

*I* is God, Self-maintained and Self-sustained, and when we are able to give up our concern for the false sense of I, the *I* that we really are goes right along enjoying itself, prospering and drawing to itself everything and everyone that it needs for its unfoldment.

As we stop resenting thrusts at the false sense of ourselves, we will no longer meet with unhappy experiences. As we give up every desire for recognition and honor, we will be losing that false sense of self, and there will be less of sinful desire and less of disease and death. But as long as there is a self that welcomes recognition and fights out against rumors about itself, gossip and slander, we are catering to a false sense of I.

We must learn to face disappointments and disgrace with the same feeling that we face adulation, honor, and fame—with utter indifference—because both disgrace and honor involve a false sense of self, not our real Self. As human beings, we deserve neither honor nor disgrace; as human beings, we deserve nothing: God alone is deserving, and God is the only one.

Knowledge of the nature of error reveals the nothingness of the evils of the world, reveals their non-power by virtue of the fact that their only claim to existence is the erroneous belief that there is a false sense of I to exist in, and act upon, and through. Without that false sense of I, where would error be? If there were no I to be sick, where would sickness be? If there were no I to sin, where would sin be? If there were no I to die, where would death be?

All these would be in exactly the same place that sound would be if there were no one to hear: the sound would not be sound. And so there would be no death, if there were not a person to die. Is it not clear then that error is that sense of person that believes that there is an I separate and apart from God? Isaiah saw this as is indicated by his words: "Is there a God beside me?"[7] In other words, what he was saying was that there is only one God, and therefore there can be only one *I*. He saw, felt, and realized no selfhood apart from God. He could not speak of himself as man because that false sense, that separate sense of selfhood, had disappeared.

It is quite possible to become emotional when talking about God, the Christ, Spirit, or Soul, and be so carried away and enthralled with the beauty of it that we completely ignore the fact that we are being eaten up by a false sense of self even while voicing all these poetic truths and beauties about God.

### *Only the False Images in Thought Are Destroyed*

When we contemplate God's allness with all its ramifications, we must reach the conclusion that that allness cannot possibly embrace a single error—no poverty, disease, age, or death. God's allness does not make God responsible for death, not even the death of our enemies. True, the *Old Testament* tells us that when God was on the field all the enemies died. It is more than likely that the prophets knew whereof they spoke, but their language, which was undoubtedly symbolic of a deeper meaning, led the people to accept and expect that the enemy literally must lie dead outside of the walls of the city. We cannot look to God to destroy our enemies unless we accept the one enemy, a false sense of self; and truth will annihilate that without any question or doubt, but it will not leave any corpses around.

Destroying anyone is never going to save our own skins because the law of as-ye-sow-so-shall-ye-reap will always and forever be in operation. Enslaving somebody else can never bring freedom. As we, individually or as a nation, do unto another, so it will be done unto us. Every country in past history that has attained glory and power through its army and navy is now in the dust, and the few remaining are on the way out. There is no possibility of evading or avoiding the karmic law. "The mills of the gods grind slowly, but they grind exceeding fine."

God is a destroyer, a destroyer of the false images in thought, but never a destroyer of persons or of conditions because there are no persons or conditions to be destroyed any more than there is a principle of mathematics which destroys the 5 at the end of 2 × 2. It is only the *belief that* 2 × 2 is 5 that is destroyed, only a false picture, not a thing or a condition. In fact, the principle does not even correct the thing or condition because there is no thing or condition to be corrected: there is only that false image in thought which looks like 5 where 4 should be.

So when we speak of all forms of error as illusion, false appearance, suggestion, or temptation, it does not mean that those things exist as externalized reality: it means that they exist in our minds which is the only place where these incorrect concepts have to be corrected.

### All Conflicts Are Within

Begin your spiritual life with the understanding that all conflicts must be settled within your consciousness.[8]

How can they be, if they exist out there in a patient, a student, or a neighbor? It would be an impossibility to settle these conflicts, if they were external to us, but the hope and the blessing is that they are not. There is no conflict going on in us, or around us, or about us that cannot be resolved within ourselves, and when it is resolved within, we shall see the outer picture change.

Anyone can prove this by considering some person toward whom he feels a deep prejudice, or who, he feels, has a deep prejudice against him and, instead of going to that person in an attempt to resolve the conflict, spending a few days or a few hours each day going inside himself and trying to understand that person from the standpoint of God. Is

God beholding anything other than its own image and likeness? As a matter of fact, does anything exist in the world
but the image and likeness of God? Is Genesis wrong when
it states that God created all that was made, and all that God
made is good? And if God made all that was made, and if all
that God made is good, then this person toward whom we
have this unpleasant feeling or who seems to have this feeling
toward us, this very person must be the image and likeness
of God, must be this same God-consciousness, this same
offspring of God, God unfolded, revealed, and disclosed.

If we keep doing that every single day until an answer-
ing response comes within us which we recognize as love,
we shall begin to experience a feeling of love and compas-
sion toward that person, and we will then not be disturbed
whether he is angry with us or not, and certainly we cannot
be angry with him. It is surprising how quickly a change will
occur.

That is a very simple thing to do once, but if we are
unfortunate enough to know twenty or thirty such persons,
it is not quite so easy because we are called upon to repeat
that process over and over and over again until it becomes
an automatic reaction. Furthermore, we have to do the same
thing not only with people, but with all the experiences of
life. There is no person or circumstance to which this does
not extend, none whatsoever.

### *There Is Only One Self*

As we believe about another, it will be believed about
us. Whatever we accept is our belief, and we must pay the
penalty for that belief. If we believe that sin, disease, and
death are the realities of existence and that there are those
suffering from them, then we must accept sin, disease, and

death for ourselves. When we understand that they exist as a false sense of existence without reality, law, cause, and without substance, then we annihilate them for those who come to us as friends, relatives, patients, or students, but we likewise annihilate them for ourselves because there is but one Self.

Whenever we are presented with the problems of the world, if we can bring ourselves to the realization that fear is at the root of them and if we can understand that fear is not a power but only a false sense of self trying to preserve itself, we shall witness some remarkable healings. By understanding the basic nature of error to be a fear about self and that actually there is only one Self, God, we do not react to the fears of our patients or our students, and they quickly become free. One person knowing the truth can set thousands of others free because what they are suffering from is the fear of a selfhood apart from God, and as long as one person knows that there is no such selfhood, he will not entertain any fear but will be free, and his being free will set others free.

There is only one Selfhood which is God, but there is a *sense* of selfhood which we all entertain and about which our fears develop. To recognize that we are suffering from nothing but a fear about ourselves and then to realize that there is no such self ties up the whole nature of error in a neat little box of nothingness.

> There is never a conflict with person or condition, but rather a false concept mentally entertained *about* person, thing, circumstance, or condition. Therefore, make the correction within yourself, rather than attempting to change anyone or anything in the without.[9]

There we have the whole of wisdom in one short sentence.

### The True Purpose of Prayer

Prayer is the inner vision of harmony. This vision is attained by giving up the desire to change or improve anyone or anything.[10]

If we take such wisdom into our work when we are called upon for healing, we instantly ask ourselves, "Is that what I am doing, or am I trying to change someone? Am I trying to change a condition?" That will correct us immediately and bring us back to truth, and we then begin to see, "Yes, that is what I have been doing. I have had a fear about this person or condition and have been trying to change it. But if I am not supposed to change a person or a condition, what am I supposed to do?"

That brings us to another of the "Wisdoms":

Prayer is an awareness of that which IS by seeing it—not making it so.

In other words, we do not make harmony by any mental or spiritual process. Harmony is brought about through prayer, which is an inner capacity to see the perfected man or universe of God. This is not possible through the senses of sight, hearing, taste, touch, or smell because the five physical senses are aware only of a false sense of man, and they cannot perceive spiritual man. We have to go beyond the thinking mind into that inner Soul-capacity, that silence where spiritual reality is revealed to us. We do not create it: it is revealed to us as already existent in spite of any appearance.

To pray is to *become aware* of the harmony without a mental effort on your part.[11]

We are not to try to make it so through any mental effort; we are not to try to create or bring about harmony any more than we would try to bring about 2 × 2 is 4. Our awareness that 2 × 2 equals 4 makes that principle operative in our experience, but the principle that 2 × 2 is 4 existed before Abraham. So, too, harmony in our experience already exists: the important point is to become aware of it; and we become aware of it, first of all, by realizing that the persons or conditions with which we are confronted are not what they appear to be. Therefore, instead of trying to change them, we go within to become acquainted with them.

The best way to do that is not to think about the person or condition, but to think about God. The moment we become acquainted with God, a miracle happens: we know our patient; we know him face to face; we know who he is, what he is, and what makes him what he is for the simple reason that having become aware of God, we have become aware of all that constitutes our patient. That which is our patient or student really and truly is God manifested. The eyes will not testify to that and neither will the hearing, taste, touch, or smell, but in that inner chamber of our being when we come face to face with God, we shall find that we have come face to face with the son of God—God the Father and God the Son.

Prayer is the absence of desire in the recognition of *IS*.[12]

Prayer is the absence of desire for person, place, thing, condition, or circumstance. Asking for parking places, automobiles, homes, or for companionship is error, but asking for illumination, for light, asking for the realization of God—asking, praying for it, knowing it, even demanding it—is right because when we are asking or even demanding that, we are really just demanding that the obstruction in our own thought be removed. We are not demanding anything of God. We are demanding that our own sense of ignorance be removed. We are really talking to ourselves when we are asking, desiring, begging, and pleading for light. We are not asking God for it because God has no more power to with-hold it than the sun has to withhold light or heat. We do pray for spiritual illumination, but what we are really praying for is that our false sense of self be removed because that is what is blocking our way to God.

Be sure that your prayer is not an attempt to influence God.[13]

We all could spend a year on that one sentence with profit. If we were to stand and watch ourselves when we are praying and meditating, would we not find a little trace of an attempt to influence God, and sometimes more than a little trace?

Have no desires in the world. Let God's grace suffice.[14]

If we can bring ourselves to that state of consciousness where we can surrender the false sense of self—the false ego that wants to be catered to, that wants to be glorified, that wants to be understood, that does not want to be slandered or gos-siped about—and when we have no desire, not even the desire to be free of gossip or slander, then God's grace will suffice. There is only one reason that gossip and slander can hurt us, and that is if we deserve them. Slander and gossip cut deeply when we are guilty, but we can be completely indifferent to them when we are not guilty.

There is an insight in man that visions through all appearances.[15]

That is the goal; that is the achievement of spiritual conscious-ness. When we rise to that place in consciousness where we see with inner vision, we will see through all appearances. We will not be fooled by a false ego that wants to be dressed up and wants to keep all of its errors hidden, but we will be willing to desire neither the good nor the evil and be satisfied to accept God's grace in the assurance that it will reveal the harmony necessary to us.

## Across the Desk

In doing world work, always remember that you are not seeking to change the conditions of "this world." Does this shock you? It should not, because now you know that "My kingdom is not of this world."[16] You also know that "My peace" is not the peace that the absence of war can give, or that health or wealth can give. "My peace" and "My kingdom" refer to a state of consciousness that is not of an earthly nature, not even of a good earthly nature.

World work in The Infinite Way consists of bringing the kingdom of God to earth. What exactly does this mean to you? To me, it means transforming my own consciousness to God-consciousness, living and moving and having my being as the Christ, and not living as mortal man. It means to mold my desires, ambitions, and actions to conform "to the pattern shewed to thee in the mount,"[17] as taught in the Sermon on the Mount.

Above all, it is to live only as *I*, knowing that *I* embody my good, to understand that the bread, meat, wine, and water of life are the substance and activity of my conscious-ness, and to know that power does not exist outside of me, and that it is not necessary to use any power.

*I am the way, and there is no other way than* I.

I *cannot fear what mortal sense does or says, for the belief in two powers is powerless to enforce itself. In* My *kingdom, nothing enters to defile because of omnipresence.* I *am the law of life, of love, and of peace. Besides* Me, *there are no other powers.*

To dwell in this consciousness or, better still, to live as this consciousness brings the kingdom of God to earth.

Failure in prayer is due primarily to trying to relate the kingdom of God to earthly conditions. We, consciously or unconsciously, try to influence spirit to change matter or people, but prayer is the realization of God *as* person and condition, not as one substance acting upon another. For example, to expect God, spirit, to bring peace on earth to "the natural man" or to the man of earth is folly. True prayer brings a change of consciousness from that of human consciousness to that mind "which was also in Christ Jesus."[18] In this higher consciousness, peace is the natural state of being. God cannot be influenced to change the health of the human race, but God realized as the health of our countenance restores the original harmony.

Praying to God for supply for yourself or for the world is a waste of time, but realizing that "the earth is the Lord's, and the fulness thereof,"[19] and "Son ... all that I have is thine"[20] restores abundance.

Prayer in world work should be based on "My kingdom is not of this world."[21] Keep your conversation in heaven; keep your prayer anchored in God and in spiritual truth. God cannot be prevailed upon to stop accidents on the highways, but the realization of God as the mind of man will reveal divine law, order, and harmony.

Let your daily world prayer be a part of your tithing, giving back to God of your first fruits.

# ✤ 9 ✤

## SPIRITUAL DOMINION

Truth is within ourselves.
There is an inmost center in us all,
Where the Truth abides in fullness; and to know
Rather consists in opening out a way
Whence the imprisoned splendour may escape
Than in effecting entry for a light supposed to be without.

—Robert Browning

PRACTICALLY ALL HUMAN experience testifies to the very opposite of Robert Browning's words. In a human sense, forces outside our own being are continually acting upon us. We are affected by weather, climate, and food; by racial, religious, and nationalistic beliefs; and by national and international economic conditions. We are acted upon by germs; we are acted upon by the belief of age, heredity, environment, and by education or the lack of it.

Because all these things are conditions or circumstances over which we apparently have no control, it is easy to blame all our ills and troubles on someone or something else. And oftentimes, if there is no person or thing on which to blame the calamities befalling us, the superstitious may resort to astrology, to looking up to the stars in an attempt to determine in what position they were on the date on which they were born, and then reach the conclusion that their problems can be laid at the door of the stars; or if they are wont to delve into the occult, they may believe that someone who has passed on has put a curse upon them.

To what ridiculous ends we go in an effort to find an alibi for our personal failures, and what weak excuses we make to ourselves and to others in order to avoid personal responsibility! As a matter of fact, in the human picture, there is only one reason for our ills, misfortunes, and discords, and that is ignorance—spiritual ignorance. We have never been taught the truth and, being in ignorance of the truth, we have had nothing with which to meet the vicissitudes of life; therefore we have become victims of persons and circumstances.

The entire human race is in the same situation. People throughout the world may really believe that they are being truthful when they claim that they are not responsible for their troubles, but that is because they have never been taught that they do not have to be victims of forces external to themselves. That is a truth which has never been taught to mankind. It is only those who have been fortunate enough to come in contact with a mystic or with mystical teaching, and who have been taught the truth of being, who know that the power to control their destiny lies within themselves, and that no person, no group of persons, no nation, conditions, or circumstances can operate to harm, destroy, or to prevent the truth from being manifested.

### Taking the Journey Back to the Father's House

The question naturally arises: Where is that truth to be found on earth? And it must be admitted that it can be found in very, very few places. If this truth be so hard to find, we must conclude that it is only those who through some inner grace are led to spiritual teaching who become immune to the things of this world. Actually, then, no one in the human picture is to blame for his troubles so long as he is ignorant of the truth of being. After he learns the truth of being, however, he can no longer put the blame for his problems on someone else in the past, the present, or at any time.

The truth of being is that God created all that was made and all that God made is good. He made man in his own image and likeness and gave him dominion over everything on the earth, in the sky above, and the sea below. Empowered with this spiritual dominion, man, the image and likeness of God, can never claim that his troubles come from anyone or any condition because he himself has been given dominion.

But the human race lost that dominion and sank to the state of the Prodigal Son who wasted his God-given heritage and ended up with the swine. The human race became enslaved, engulfed by war, depressions, poverty, disease, and sin, all because of surrendering its dominion through ignorance of its true identity.

All this is the prodigal state which continues to be a part of the human experience until the individual, like the Prodigal Son in Scripture, begins to wonder, "Is this the way life is meant to be? Why, even the servants in my Father's house are better off than I am." Then he begins to work his way back to the Father's house and, as he approaches, he is robed with the cloak of divine grace and given the ring of divine authority. Once again he finds himself in possession of the dominion bestowed on him at birth.

So when a person discovers a spiritual teaching that puts him on the spiritual path, it will ultimately bring him back to the truth that dominion is within himself. Immediately, then, he loses the fear of "man, whose breath is in his nostrils."[1] He begins to realize:

*I shall not fear any conditions existing in the world, for I and the Father are one, and that Father is greater than he that is in the world. The Father within me doeth the works.*

When a person perceives this truth, he has already begun the long journey back to the Father's house where he will once again become conscious of his God-given dominion. Then he will not fear people—individually or collectively— or conditions or circumstances, for he knows that he is master of these by right of his God-given dominion.

### The Power Within

The basis of all mystical teaching is: "I and my Father are one.[2] ... Son, thou art ever with me, and all that I have is thine."[3] To take these passages into consciousness and abide with them, living with them day after day, restores to an individual the awareness that the grace of God has been bestowed upon him and that, because of that grace, he has dominion. The moment the student ponders the idea, "*I* have dominion," the word *I* begins to work in his consciousness, and then he remembers: "I will never leave thee, nor forsake thee.[4] ... Lo, I am with you alway, even unto the end of the world.[5] ... If I make my bed in hell, behold, thou art there.[6] ... Though I walk through the valley of the shadow of death, I will fear no evil: for thou art with me."[7]

So the student begins to realize the nature of that word *I:*

*I in the midst of me is mighty. "I am the way, the truth, and the life.[8] ... I am the bread of life.[9] ... I am the resurrection and the life."[10] This I within me, this I, this truth, this grace of God, this son of God, this oneness with God—this is my bread and my wine and my water, and therefore I understand what the Master meant when he said: "Take no thought for your life, what ye shall eat, or what ye shall drink; nor yet for your body, what ye shall put on."* [11]

*What the Master really was saying is: "Do not pray for supply: I am the bread; I am the wine; I am the water. Do not take thought for anything concerning your human life, for I am the substance of it and the activity of it. Dwell only in Me, in the realization that I abide in you, that I really am you. I constitute your being—I. I in the midst of you is your grace, the grace of God unto you."*

*I need not look to "man, whose breath is in his nostrils"[12] for anything; I need not fear what mortal man can do to me. I need not plot and plan and plunder, for this I that I am, this divine presence, this he that is within me, this it goes before me to make the crooked places straight. It prepares a place for me: it walks beside me; it walks behind me as a rear guard; it goes with me whithersoever I go.*

"He that abideth in me, and I in him, the same bringeth forth much fruit."[13] Does the Master say that this has to be only in time of prosperity or in peacetime, or does he say plainly and unequivocally: "He that abideth in me, and I in him, the same bringeth forth much fruit"? Wherever we are, whether it is in heaven or hell or in the valley of the shadow of death, wherever it is and whenever it is: "*I* will never leave you, nor forsake you. When you go through the waters or through the flames, you will not drown, nor will the flames kindle upon you, for *I* am with you." This divine power which is God in action—the son of God in us, the God-being, the divine presence within all of us, the he within us—is greater than any circumstance or condition of the outer world.

So when a Pilate of any name or nature says to us, "I can crucify you," quick as a flash our reply should be, "'Thou couldest have no power at all against me, except it were given thee from above.'[14] There is no power outside of me that can act upon me. *All* power is within me acting upon this world. This power within me can still the storm, and can prevent any enemy from touching me because it reveals that there is no power and no enemy without. All power is given unto me from on High."

## *Deny Thyself*

The spiritually awakened person realizes that God's grace is his sufficiency in all things and for all things: food, clothing, health, harmony, protection, safety, security, peace, companionship, and home. Such an enlightened person no longer looks to man for supply, for companionship, or for home, but is willing to share the supply, companionship, and home he has. He does not look to anyone or believe that it is his right to receive these from anyone, but having returned now to the Father-consciousness and become dead to himself, dead to personal self, personality, and personal possessions, he comes to the realization that "the earth is the Lord's, and the fulness thereof,"[15] and that all that the Father has is his. Therefore, instead of seeking things or persons, he now seeks to share and to give. It is an *outflow* rather than a seeking for an *inflow*. He is now living in this truth:

*Truth does not come to me: it is within me. Supply, infinite supply, God-supply, is within me. It does not come to me: it flows out from me. The companionship of God is within me—it does not come to me—and all I seek is to share that companionship which God has given me.*

A dry seed of itself is nothing and never can be anything in its seed state. Only when it gives itself up, surrenders itself, and permits itself to be broken open by the natural elements, does the seed change its form and eventually become a whole tree full of fruit. So it is that we—insignificant you and I, who of ourselves are really nothing—suddenly become the source through which flows infinite wisdom, love, companionship, supply, forgiveness, and infinite good in every form.

Jesus was quick to admit that of his own self he was nothing, but we all know what has gone out through him to this world because of that very denial of self and the acknowledgment that it was the spirit of the Father that did the work. It is much the same with us because as long as we insist on living to ourselves, trying to be something and claiming something, we will be just a seed. How different life becomes for us when we are willing to deny ourselves and admit that of ourselves we are nothing and can do nothing, but that through the Christ we can do all things!

Think what Saul of Tarsus was—less than nothing. Then think what St. Paul was, and you will see how a little nothing of a Saul became the great light Paul. Think how unimportant Jesus must have been as a Hebrew rabbi; then recall how great he became as the founder of Christianity. As a rabbi with an established position in the world, he might have been tempted to look upon himself as something. It was only when he perceived that he was nothing that he became all.

One of the first realizations that comes to every person who has a spiritual experience is his unimportance as a person. How small a part an individual can play in the world's history by means of his own human capacity! But suddenly in that nothingness and seemingly from nowhere, the light dawns, and something begins to flow out from within him to the whole world! When that happens, a Gautama becomes the Buddha, a Jesus becomes the Christ, a Saul becomes

Paul, a John becomes the Revelator. A shoemaker, Jacob Boehme, uneducated, a nobody, becomes the father of a long line of mystics. From a shoemaker to a mystic! Brother Lawrence who wrote that masterpiece *Practicing the Presence of God*—Brother Lawrence, a nothing, a nobody, a monk in a monastery, cooking for other monks—has lived in history for hundreds of years. Walt Whitman, a little insignificant printer in a print shop, is one of the half dozen people of his generation who has survived in the minds of men and been accepted throughout the world as a great mystic.

The very moment that the spirit of the Lord God touches an individual, he becomes the son of God. Paul says: "They that are in the flesh cannot please God ... but as many as are led by the spirit of God, they are the sons of God.[16] ... Therefore, if any man be in Christ, he is a new creature: old things are passed away; behold, all things are become new."[17] Then he becomes the son of God; he becomes less than he was of himself; and then this light goes before him and it either gives to the world some new religious teaching or some new way of practicing an old religious teaching, or it produces something new or greater in music, art, or literature. But in one way or another, it is always the power of the presence that does it.

## Practice and Not Conversation

To help us learn how to become the sons of God and to experience the flow of this power, we should begin to live and apply the promises of Scripture until they become flesh of our flesh, blood of our blood, bone of our bone, until they become so much a part of us that we become the truth. Truth itself dwells in us, feeding us and all those who come to us.

Then we no longer blame anyone or anything; we no longer criticize, judge, or condemn anyone, any group, any nationality, or any race or religion. But we accept the responsibility which comes through knowing that "I and my Father are one,"[18] that all that the Father has is ours, and that he that is within us is greater than he that is in the world. Once that is acknowledged within us, we then have to begin to live and to practice it.

*The kingdom of God is within me. Through the grace of God, I can feed multitudes, I can share supply, companionship, friendship, service—all good. From the infinity which is my being, I can begin to pour out, rather than to expect someone or something in the external to provide for my needs.*

Every day we must practice letting infinity flow out from us, even though it be giving only a penny or a bit of service here or there, or sharing a few moments of companionship. If, for any reason, there are those who are unable to do that, they can begin to share forgiveness. They can look out at the everpresent world of enemies—personal, national, racial— and begin to forgive them, praying that God's mercy open their consciousness. They can begin to pray, not so much for their friends and relatives, but for the sick and the sinning of the world, for those who are downtrodden, dejected, and rejected.

One reaction to such a program may be, "Oh, but I'm further down in the scale than are these people for whom I am supposed to pray." In this realization, we forget that: we give what we have to give, and if we have nothing to give but prayer, then we pray. If we have nothing to give but forgiveness, we give forgiveness. If we have nothing to give but service or dedication, we give it—but we *give!*

This is a practice. This is not conversation; this is not reading a book and exclaiming, "How lovely!" This is taking it out of the book and putting it into practice. In other words, it is acknowledging that infinity dwells within, and if we have only one dollar's worth of infinity at this minute let us give ten cent's worth of it away. It makes no difference how little we may have at the moment. What counts is that we make the acknowledgment that infinity is the measure of our being and act as though that were true, even though we act only with pennies, or if we act only with forgiveness or prayers or service.

The way of the spiritual life was presented to the world by the Master, and that is why he is called the way-shower: "I came down from heaven, not to do mine own will, but the will of him that sent me."[19] He practiced doing the will of the Father by healing and feeding the multitudes, forgiving sin, praying for the enemy, and by teaching the lessons which he had learned of God. If he is the way-shower, then we have to follow the way he showed us, and that way is the way of acknowledging that while we of our own selves are nothing, all that the Father has is ours, and we can begin to share that allness.

### *The World Loses Its Hold on Us*

It will not take too long a period of this kind of practice before things begin to come into our experience which prove to us that we have regained some measure of dominion, that now the world is not doing to us quite the same things it formerly did, and certainly not doing them to us in quite so hard a way. Eventually, we realize, "The world is dead to me; it can do nothing to me or for me. 'My kingdom is not of this world.'[20] Therefore, it has nothing good to give me, and there is nothing evil that it can do to me. This world has nothing for me, for my kingdom is a spiritual kingdom, and I receive my good from the spiritual source."

Too many truth-students believe that their study should bring them more material good, so they continue to dwell in "this world," only now they are dwelling in the good aspects of it instead of the bad. But they have not yet reached the kingdom, and they never will reach the kingdom until they are dead to this world, or as the Master phrased it, until they have "overcome this world."

There may be some truth-students who are not ready to go so far on the spiritual path as to be willing to give up the good things of this world, or even to acknowledge that they should not be seeking health, happiness, and abundance through the spirit. Interestingly enough, however, being in the world but not of it does not mean asceticism: it does not involve sackcloth and ashes; it does not involve living in poverty or in hovels—not at all.

We can be in this world and use all of its good, and yet not be dependent on it, or even desire it, but as it takes place in our experience stand by watching and let it be of use and help to us. In other words, there is nothing of good that this world can do for us, and there is nothing of evil that it can do because although we are in this world, we are not of it.

As we come to that place in consciousness where we are not trying to use God to attain some form of human good, but where we accept the Master's revelation that we are to seek only the kingdom of God, we shall then find that the good things of the earth are added to us, and they do play a part in our experience.

## Dwelling in the Kingdom

The real beginning is made when we can accept the revelation that the kingdom of God is within us, when we begin to realize that this divine grace which is the presence and power of God in us can, does, and will supply us with everything necessary to our unfoldment, and when we come to that place where we no longer not only do not blame anyone for our troubles, but no longer dwell on them.

When this truth has been realized in some measure, we take the second step which is one of sharing. We no longer look for companionship, but rather give companionship; we no longer seek supply, but share supply; we no longer seek to gain, but seek only to be that instrument through which God's grace flows to this world.

Ultimately, we come to the experience described by Paul: "I live; yet not I, but Christ liveth in me."[21] It is then that the student touches one of the very high rungs of the ladder of the spiritual life. Without effort, without labor, and without toil and sweat, divine inspiration is always at work within, performing that which is given him to do, and he can, therefore, do it without strife, without struggle, and without even a fear of failure because even though he may seem to be doing it, it is not really he that is performing it but the *he* that is within him, and he himself is but the instrument through which it is being performed.

It makes no difference whether his work is giving forth a truth-message or being the instrument for healing, or whether it is in music, art, literature, bridge building, or newspaper publishing. It makes no difference what the work is: there is this spiritual intuition at work within one to perform it, to provide the inspiration, the wisdom, the knowledge, and the power, even to draw unto one the very capital that may be needed for the particular enterprise. After realizing that the presence within is the power unto all things, one finds that everything comes by the grace of God.

Actually, the teaching of Jesus is a teaching of individual responsibility. In other words, our daily outer experience—success or failure—is the effect or result of the activity of our own consciousness. Therefore, the degree in which we are willing to abide in the Word and let the Word abide in us is the degree of harmony on the outer plane, and so if we decide to set aside a half-hour a day for truth, we can count upon one forty-eighth of a day of perfect harmony. And if we decide that one hour is the measure of truth we will take in, we can expect one twenty-fourth of a day of peace, joy, and love.

When we come to the place of praying without ceasing, living in the Word, letting the Word live in us, abiding in the Word and letting the Word abide in us, dwelling in the secret place of the most High, living and moving and having our being in the consciousness of truth, we can look forward, then, to about twenty-three twenty-fourths of a day of harmony. There is always a little bit left for the future—we do not ever quite attain complete fulfillment. Jesus attained his fulfillment only after the Resurrection, and we, too, may first have to be entombed in our troubles and resurrected out of them before we attain the fullness of the God-head bodily.

## ACROSS THE DESK

The Infinite Way is dedicated to revealing innate, individual, spiritual freedom which appears as freedom from bondage to the senses: to the body, to the purse, and to circumstances. Acquiring some knowledge of truth is the raft on which we travel to *"My* kingdom" where all receive freedom, peace, and immortality. There is a story from the Chinese to the effect that when a person travels and comes to a deep stream, he builds a raft and crosses the stream on it, but once he is on land again he drops the raft and leaves it behind lest it become a burden to him. So do we use the letter of truth as a raft to carry us across the river of our ignorance. Then, upon reaching *"My* kingdom," we drop the letter of truth and clothe ourselves with the spirit, thus attaining freedom.

Our real freedom is not freedom *from* anything, but a freedom in Christ which *appears* as freedom from fear, from the body, from the purse, and from limitation of every nature:

Every human being will demonstrate the continuity of life after death, but only the spiritually free attain immortality.

Every human being may achieve health, abundance, and a measure of happiness, but only the spiritually free attain life by grace—"not by might nor by power," but by the realization of omnipresence.

Almost every human being believes in God, but only those enlightened through the continuous realization of omnipresence attain the grace of God in daily life and experience.

Few ideas contain the inherent power of spiritual freedom that is found in the constant remembrance of the words, "Emmanuel, or God with us." To *live* in the continuous awareness of Emmanuel is to float on a safe raft into *"My* kingdom," the realm of eternal freedom and peace.

Sing the song, "Emmanuel, God with us," morning, noon, and night, and cross the river of ignorance to *"My* kingdom," and know forever *"My* peace."

# ❖ 10 ❖

## THE MEANING OF PRAYER

FOR MANY YEARS after the Crucifixion, the majority of Jesus' followers resisted all efforts that were made to bring them into conformity with the teachings of the Master. They continued to live by the Hebraic laws, many of them insisting that no Gentiles be admitted to their brotherhood, that all men must be circumcised, and that all members observe their dietary rules. It was only years later, with the advent of Paul and his teaching of "neither circumcision availeth anything, nor uncircumcision,"[1] that the Judaic laws were dropped and the Christian teaching accepted.

Today, too, we find that it is not easy to give up teachings and traditions of our childhood, regardless of how erroneous they may have been, and we therefore often continue to cling to them throughout our lives. I well remember the day when my mother told me that there was no Santa Claus and that there was no use hanging up my stocking on Christmas Eve. No Santa Claus! I knew better than my mother. I was not going to believe it for a minute; therefore, I proceeded to hang up my stocking. Even my mother could not break a belief that had been implanted in me from the time I came on earth. I was looking forward to Santa Claus coming on Christmas and bringing me a whole tree full of gifts, and no one was going to take that away from me.

So, also, do we cling to our early religious teachings relative to the nature of God. God has been set up as a kind of superhuman parent to whom we can go and cry, asking for what we want, and if we just cry hard enough, sacrifice, tithe, light a candle, take off our shoes, put our hats on, or perform some other ritual, we may get what we ask for. Each group or denomination has its own way of persuading God to do its will; each one has some way in which it tries to appease God and thereby hopes that God will open up his bag of gifts and hand out health to one, supply to another, a husband to one, a divorce to another, or a child to one, and so on and on and on.

This is based on the belief that God has something that he is withholding and that he is not going to give it up until we manage to wheedle him into the right frame of mind, or until we succeed in pleasing him in some way or other. Surely, in our spiritual adulthood, we must know that there can be no such God, because to entertain such a concept of God is to humanize Deity.

It is not easy to take a Santa-Claus-God away from people who still expect that God is going to do something for them if they tithe, if they are sanctimonious or look holy. That is a difficult habit of thought to break; nevertheless it has to be broken. God is omnipresent wherever we are, and we do not have to roll our eyes up to him or make a pretense of being good to receive his blessings.

### Our State of
### Consciousness Returns to Us

Let us get over the idea that there is a rewarding or a punishing God. There is no God to reward or to punish anybody for anything. God is not a man or a woman; God has no human instincts. God is spirit and God is love, and when we remember how parents love their bad children as well as their good ones, how much less cognizance must God take of goodness or of badness!

It is true that we do receive punishment for our wrongdoing, but from what source does that punishment come? The punishment is never from God: it is from the state of consciousness that brought about the sin. In other words, if we believe that we lack to such an extent that we are willing to steal to satisfy our needs, it is our belief in lack that is punishing us; or if we think that taking somebody else's property can enrich us, we are going to suffer from that belief because we cannot avoid suffering from what we accept in our consciousness.

Whatsoever we mete out, that is the way it is going to be measured back to us—not by God, but by our own sins, by our own state of consciousness. It is the state of consciousness that we express that returns to us. The bread that we cast upon the water is the bread that returns to us. So it is important that we cast fresh bread with good fresh butter on it, for it is going to come right back to us, and if we have not put good out, there is no good to come back to us.

## Praying for Spiritual Bread

The Master made it clear that God has no pleasure in our sacrifices. He also made it clear that man was not made for the Sabbath, but that the Sabbath was made for man, that worshiping in holy mountains, or even in holy temples, has no value, and above all things he made it clear that we should take no thought for our life, what we should eat, or what we should drink, or wherewithal we should be clothed, and he may even have gone on and added, "housed," too.

It is true that over and over again he said, "Ask, and it shall be given you; seek, and ye shall find; knock, and it shall be opened unto you,"[2] but he also explained what we were to ask for: bread, and he told us what "bread" is. The bread that he was talking about had no relationship to baker's bread or to the kind a cook or housewife can turn out; the bread to which he referred was the bread of life; and he said, "*I* am the bread of life."[3]

Not long ago after a lecture, someone totally unfamiliar with The Infinite Way came up to me and said, "I can go along with you in most things, but not with what you say about prayer. You say that we must not pray to God for anything, but Jesus prayed, 'Give us this day our daily bread.'[4]"

And I replied, "Yes, I can understand your feeling that way, but probably no one has ever explained to you what bread is. Just what is bread? Jesus said, and nearly every Christian church repeats this in its communion service, 'I am the bread.'[5]"

He wondered why he had never seen this before, but it was because he had read the Bible with the conditioning he had received in his childhood and from his early religious teaching, and not with an unconditioned mind. Somebody had perhaps pointed out this passage and told this man what he understood it to mean, and that is as far as he had ever gone. That is the way with many of us: we have accepted our childhood teachings, never questioning them and never realizing that we ought to think for ourselves.

Thus it is that when we pray for daily bread, we are to remember what bread is and that we are praying for Christly substance which is understanding, praying for the spirit of God to be in us, praying that light be given to us, that God's grace be made evident to us, praying as though we really understood the Master's teaching of two thousand years ago that the kingdom of God is within us:

*Father, even though I know that the kingdom of God is within me, reveal it to me now. If I have forgotten this great truth, if the mesmerism of human living has separated me from it, open my eyes that I may see, open my ears that I may hear.*

All we have to do is to turn within and pray, but not as though we were praying to a human being, to a human mother or father who has a piece of candy to give us, a toy, or a new dress. To pray in that way is to humanize God. It is trying to make God over into the image and likeness of a Santa Claus, but we may as well know, once and for all time, that our God is not in the business of putting presents under Christmas trees—not even for good children.

God *is*—this we must know. God is good—this, too, we must know. And God is closer to us than breathing and nearer than hands and feet—this we also must know. The Master further stated that God knows our needs and that it is his good pleasure to give us the kingdom. Let us, therefore, stop begging, asking, and seeking for things, and seek "first the kingdom of God, and his righteousness."[6] The only legitimate asking, seeking, and knocking is that which we direct within ourselves.

## Laying up Spiritual Treasures

The whole basis of prayer in The Infinite Way is that we cannot pray for anything to come to us because in the beginning, "before Abraham was," God established the whole kingdom within us. Nothing can be added to us, but we can pray that the kingdom of God, which is within us, find expression and outlet through us. It is much like turning to our memory in order to bring to mind some fact which has escaped us, and we bring it forth from within ourselves even though temporarily we had lost sight of the fact that we knew it.

So it is with any form of good. It cannot come to us: it must flow out from us. Many of us have experienced temporary forms of good that have come to us apparently for no reason at all. Sometimes money, position, and fame have been almost thrust upon us, but because we have not brought them forth from within ourselves, they do not really belong to us, and very often we have the sad and unpleasant experience of finding out that they really were not ours because they were not the fruitage of our consciousness and, therefore, they were not permanent.

That which we bring forth from within our own consciousness, we will never lose. As a matter of fact, we will take it with us when we leave this scene. Jesus was not indulging in fanciful poetic language when he said, "Lay not up for yourselves treasures upon earth, where moth and rust doth corrupt, and where thieves break through and steal: But lay up for yourselves treasures in heaven, where neither moth nor rust doth corrupt, and where thieves do not break through nor steal."[7] This is great wisdom; this is a divine principle of life which should be heeded. It does not mean that we should not have money, and have it by the billions, if it flows to us. What it means is that we should not store it up in the sense that it is our supply or that we are dependent upon it, because after all the barns and storehouses have been filled and then we build more and fill those, what are we going to do with them? Eventually, they must all be left at the door of the probate court.

We cannot take our wardrobes or our jewels with us, our storehouses or barns; we cannot take our money or any worldly possessions with us. What then have we to take with us? How do we go forth, and with what? The answer is that if we have not stored up spiritual treasures, we go out of this world a blank, and when we enter the next life, we may have to start off on a lower level than when we came into this world. It is the spiritual treasures that we have laid up in our consciousness through prayer that we carry with us wherever we go, and those treasures will ensure that our entry into the next life experience will be on a higher plane than the level on which we came into this one.

## God Is Not Responsible for Evil

God is not to be prayed to in the sense of praying to him to do, give, or bestow something on someone at some time. There is no such God. In the last war, hundreds of thousands of families prayed for the safety and the security of their sons at war, but their prayers were primarily personal and selfish, concerned only with the safety of their own, and many of those fathers and mothers lost their sons in one way or another.

Does this not show how useless it is to go to God for anything of a personal and selfish nature and to believe that there is a God who cares whether we are of one country or another, whether we are Jew or Gentile, Protestant or Catholic, Buddhist or Moslem? What kind of God would make a distinction between one racial, national, or religious group and another?

As a matter of fact, in order to overcome the religious superstitions people have accepted, we must eventually overcome the belief that God cares more for good people than for bad people. All we have to do is to travel this world for a while to find out that the good people are suffering just as much as the bad people: they have just as many colds and just as much cancer, tuberculosis, and polio. Even innocent little children suffer before they know enough to be either good or bad. God is not holding innocent children in condemnation, or innocent men and women, and letting the rascals go free. God has no part in any of that. God is not responsible for evil.

God does not enter the human scene until an individual returns to him. In the fifteenth chapter of John, the Master taught: "If ye abide in me, and my words abide in you, ye shall ask what ye will, and it shall be done unto you."[8] But if you do not abide in this Word, if you do not let this Word abide in you, you will be "cast forth as a branch and [be] withered."[9] There we have it! It does not say on which side of the boundary line we are; it does not say which uniform we are wearing, which church we are entering, or what the color of our skin is: it says that we either abide in the word of God and let the word of God abide in us, or we are cut off, and it makes no difference whether we are humanly good or humanly bad, humanly white or humanly black.

Isaiah says, "Thou wilt keep him in perfect peace, whose mind is stayed on thee."[10] No distinction is made. The only requisite is to keep our mind stayed on God and thereby bring God into our experience. God fills all space, but God is available only where the mind is stayed on God, where the presence of God is maintained in consciousness, and where contact is made with him.

## The Prayer of Acknowledgment

When we begin to perceive the nature of God, we will know how to pray. When we know how to pray, all of God's grace will manifest itself in our life because prayer is the connecting link between man and God. It is through prayer that we bring God's grace into our individual experience and are enabled to share it with others so that they, too, benefit in some degree by the grace that we have received.

The Master said, "The Spirit of the Lord God is upon me, because he hath anointed me to preach the gospel to the poor; he hath sent me to heal the brokenhearted, to preach deliverance to the captives, and recovering of sight to the blind, to set at liberty them that are bruised."[11] Wherever a person makes contact with the spirit of God, in some degree he, too, is anointed, not necessarily to do healing work—some will comfort, some will support and supply, and some will bless in other ways—but in one way or another, everyone who has been ordained of God and who has received the spirit of God in him is at the same time ordained to bless and bring blessings to others.

As human beings, we are imbued neither with the life nor the wisdom of God: we do not receive the blessings of God, nor do we come under the law of God, until, at some moment of our experience, the spirit of God dwells in us, and then do we become the children of God, and as children, heirs, and as heirs, joint-heirs of Christ—"if so be that the Spirit of God dwell in [us]."[12] Then, prayer becomes an acknowledgment:

*The very place whereon I stand is holy ground. Here where I am, God is. If I mount up to heaven, God is there; if I make my bed in hell, God is there; if "I walk through the valley of the shadow of death, I will fear no evil,"[13] for God is there. Wherever I am, God is—up in the heavens, down in the hells, walking the earth, even in "the valley of the shadow of death."*

*Where God is, I am; and all that the Father has is mine. God can set a table for me in the wilderness.*

*"The heavens declare the glory of God, and the firmament sheweth his handiwork"* [14]*—and man is his greatest creation.*

*That very place where God stands, stand I, for I and the Father are one: God, the Father; God, the Son—here, where I am. Underneath me are the "everlasting arms."*

*"I will never leave thee, nor forsake thee.*[15] *... Before Abraham was, I am,"*[16] *and that I Am is with me, and that I will be with me to the end of the world; it will never leave me, nor forsake me. I can never die because that I is my life eternal. "Whither thou goest, I will go"*[17]*—whithersoever I go, God goes with me, inseparable, indivisible—one.*

When we have prayed that kind of prayer, we can rest in quietness and in confidence. Then we can listen for a moment or two as the answer comes from within. Always something wells up from within to bring assurance that this word of God is true, and that there is a presence that is ever within us, and yet that goes before us to make the crooked places straight and to prepare mansions for us.

This kind of prayer never comes down to the level of dishonoring God by implying that God is withholding something from us and that we must use some coercive method to persuade him to let loose of it.

### Prayer Reveals the
### Eternal Relationship of Oneness

God is the same yesterday, today, and forever. What God does is from everlasting to everlasting: there is no beginning to God, and there is no ending to God. Therefore, it is useless to expect God to do something for us today that he did not do yesterday.

God's work is done. When there seems to be an absence of health, harmony, wholeness, completeness, or perfection, our attitude should be not that God is withholding any of these things and that he must do something that he is not already doing to bring them to us, but rather should we accept the fact that a *sense* of separation has sprung up between God and us, and we are therefore going back to the kingdom of God within us to re-establish our sense of oneness—not to re-establish oneness because that is, always has been, and always will be intact. The human mesmerism that was brought about by accepting the belief in two powers has created a sense of separation from God which, at times, is so great that it makes us feel that God is a billion miles away upward, and we are a billion miles away downward, and that there is no possibility of spanning the gap.

Actually, this is not true. "I and my Father are one" is an eternal relationship, but if we have forgotten it, if the mesmerism of world beliefs has taken it away from us, then we have to go back within ourselves, where eventually we shall find the kingdom of God, and there, pray, ask, and knock:

*Father, reveal thyself. Break this mesmeric sense that I may pierce the veil of separation. Open my eyes that I may see; open my ears that I may hear. Glorify thou me with the glory that I had with thee in the beginning.*

Then we are not asking God for anything. What we are trying to do through this prayer is to break that mesmeric sense within ourselves until the glory of God, which is already established within us, can once more be evident in manifestation. Truth, light, love, happiness, joy, peace, dominion, companionship, home—all these are established within us. Our only task is to let them flow out from us.

The way of doing this differs with each individual. There are some who have developed such love of money and such great fear of the lack of it that it is only with reluctance that they can part with it. They may have to open a way for the infinity of God to flow forth into expression by being willing to take a few dollars and begin to give them out without fear, with a sense that these dollars belong to God, and they are going to share them.

With some persons, the thing that they are not letting flow out from them is less tangible. They may have to learn to pray for their enemies or for those who persecute them or despitefully use them, and above all to forgive even unto seventy times seven in order that they may be the children of their Father which is in heaven. There are others who have developed a pseudo-loyalty to their nation or church, and they will have to learn the meaning of the true brotherhood Jesus taught when he said, "Call no man your father upon the earth: for one is your Father, which is in heaven."[18] God is not a sectarian God, a nationalistic or a racial God.

We must make sure that we are fulfilling the demands of the Master, and even if we have to wear out our kneecaps on the ground in order to do it, we must bring ourselves to the place where we understand that God knows no such thing as boundaries, nationalities, races, or creeds, that none of those things has a place in the kingdom of God.

In that kingdom, there is no race or creed of any nature: there is only the relationship of God and his son, universal and intact. If we have any other idea of God, we shall have to work to eliminate it from our consciousness, and this we will be able to do when we learn the true nature of God and realize that God cares just as much for the daisies in the field as for the orchids, for the blades of grass as for the most luscious of fruits. God is the same to all those who bring themselves under the reign of God.

## The Humility of True Prayer

There is no way to pray other than to make of oneself a stillness, a quietness, a peacefulness, and a listening ear.

Prayer that contains words and thoughts meant to reach God is not really prayer at all. True prayer has neither words nor thoughts because it has no desires except one: to know God's will, to know him aright, to be a fitting instrument for his grace. With that one exception, prayer is desireless. It is a desireless state of being which opens the way for God's will to be known and made evident.

Prayer is an inner stillness that waits for God's thoughts— "for my thoughts are not your thoughts, neither are your ways my ways."[19] Therefore, let us be still with our thoughts and our ways, and let us hear God's thoughts and, by listening, let us come to know God's ways:

> *"Thou wilt keep him in perfect peace, whose mind is stayed on thee."*[20] *Thou wilt keep me in perfect peace in proportion as my mind is stayed on thee. Thou leadest me beside the still waters. Thou makest me to lie down in green pastures.*
>
> *What must I do? Only acknowledge that because the Lord is my shepherd I need not fear. He feedeth me in the wilderness and setteth a table before me. My function is not to tell that all-knowing intelligence, but rather to listen and be still.*

Prayer is acknowledging God as omnipotence, omniscience, and omnipresence—all-power, all-knowledge, and all-presence. Prayer is being still so that omnipotence may establish itself in our consciousness, omniscience impart itself to us, and omnipresence reveal its presence to us. Prayer does not bring God to us. Prayer does not bring God's grace to us. prayer reveals God and God's grace to be active where we are.

The most important part of prayer is that listening or receptive attitude which is a state of pure humility:

> *Speak, Lord; your servant is listening. I am not turning to you to have you do my will, as though you were my servant and*

*I could direct you to provide me with supply, health, home, or companionship. I am not coming to you as though I had greater wisdom than you and, therefore, knew what to pray for. I come to you in true humility, for I realize that I can of my own self do nothing. I do not even know how to pray, or what to pray for.*

*Therefore, Father, let your spirit make intercession with my spirit Speak, Lord, that your will may be made manifest in my experience. You are my shepherd; I shall never want. Your grace is my sufficiency in all things.*

And so in this state of receptivity, in this state of opening ourselves in humility to the will and the grace of God—whether it happens the first day or the hundred and first day is not important—eventually it happens, and we are filled with the spirit of God. There is an inner warmth, an inner stillness, an inner peace. Sometimes there is even the still small voice assuring us, "I have never left you. I will never leave you," or sometimes, "I am your bread and your wine and your water." It does not make any difference whether it comes in words, whether it comes in thoughts, or whether it comes just as a feeling, a sensing, or a release. But it is an assurance:

*God is closer to me than breathing and nearer than hands and feet. He knows my need before I do, and it is his good pleasure to give me the kingdom.*

Prayer is attunement, at-one-ment, with God. Through prayer, our eternal relationship with the Father is revealed. But for that oneness to become realized consciousness, we must go to the throne of God pure of heart, free of desires, with every barrier removed, seeking only communion, and praying the prayer of acknowledgment. In that purity, selflessness, and desirelessness, we enter the inner sanctuary, and from that high point of vision behold his kingdom on earth as it is in heaven.

## ACROSS THE DESK

Life really begins for a person when he faces fairly and squarely these questions: Why am I on earth? What came I here to do? Is there a goal to be attained? Have I begun to fulfill God's plan for me on earth? Until the beginning of such self-questioning, one's life is like that of a vegetable.

Each person has a unique destiny in life, but only a few have concerned themselves with their destiny, and fewer still have attained any awareness of their real Self. Because of this, men are sheep and follow leaders, occasionally to a better way of life, but more often to their own destruction.

It is true that labor unions have given workmen better wages and greater security, and that civil service employment has provided economic security of a sort, but this has at times stultified ambition and initiative and has been coupled with such a sacrifice of individuality that it has imprisoned the spirit of adventure, pioneering, and of achievement. To have become a power in the religious, political, or economic world tends, too, to limit one's freedom of choice, decision, movement, and growth.

In countries throughout the world, millions have died that others might survive in order to pass on to coming generations political and economic freedom, but often, after this sacrifice, the survivors have immediately imprisoned themselves in new forms. Men have fought for what they believed would result in religious freedom only to find themselves bound more securely in mental slavery. The unthinking masses fight because they follow leaders who promise liberty, justice, and equality, not knowing that even victory may mean greater serfdom and domination under still more autocratic leaders.

At some time or other, if we are not already conditioned to serving out the balance of our time on earth as vegetables, we begin to question the meaning of life, and soon receive answers which set in motion the process of freeing us. Those of us who reach the stage of self-questioning soon learn that the only wars that can be fought and won are those that take place within ourselves. Our first awakening reveals that our mind, conditioned as it is to superstition and tradition, is the prison-house in which we dwell. Then begins the warfare within ourselves between truth and error, the warfare that can result, if we are faithful, in the attainment of our complete freedom and the ability to help others.

Of all the blessings in heaven or on earth, the greatest of these is freedom. Those who would be free—physically, mentally, morally, financially, politically, and religiously— must be willing to face the truth that only the attainment of spiritual illumination will bring that freedom, and this enlightenment must take place within the consciousness of the individual.

In proportion as we attain some measure of transcendental consciousness, and only as we seek and find an inner grace, do we discover our freedom, peace, and joy, and experience outer harmony. By human means, we cannot bring peace and abundance to our world, or intelligence and integrity to those who govern.

"My kingdom is not of this world." "My peace" is not the peace that worldly conditions can give, and yet when we discover "My kingdom" and attain "My peace," we do bring some measure of its reign to earth.

The great attainment is the awareness of the nature of life and our reason for being, the awareness of the nature of the Self and of the purpose of the individual.

If there are earthly fetters still binding us, we must cease fighting them, put up our sword, and begin here and now to undertake the transformation of consciousness that brings freedom and peace to Soul, mind, and body, begin to seek the awareness of the presence within us, that presence that has been with us since "before Abraham was" and whose function it is to reveal to us "My kingdom," "My peace," and "My grace."

The natural man, or human self, does not evolve into Christhood. The spiritual man is a separate being, newborn as the "old man" is put off through the renewal of consciousness.

# ❖ 11 ❖

## BREAKING THE BONDS
## OF HUMANHOOD

THE GOAL OF ALL SPIRITUAL work is God-realization, arriving at a place where we are consciously aware that we are not living our own life, that there is a something, a transcendental presence, that has taken over, that goes before us, and that cares for us. Life eternal and divine harmony come to us in proportion as we know God aright.

While this is the most difficult part of our spiritual journey, because it involves releasing every concept of God acquired throughout our lifetime, nevertheless, it has to be the first part of it. We have looked to our concepts of God to bless us, but concepts of God, regardless of how lofty they may be, cannot bless anyone. We can be spiritually blessed only as we come to know him as he is, and that knowing has no relationship whatsoever to any concept of God. It is useless to try to define or analyze God, or to seek to know what he is through the mind. If it were possible to embrace God in our mind, God would be smaller than our mind, and this he cannot be.

One way in which we can begin to lose our concepts of God is through contemplation and meditation on the nature of God. Knowing the nature of God is quite different from knowing God itself, just as our individual nature is different from the essence that we really are. Our nature is the outward expression, or set of qualities which we possess, but we ourselves are greater than our qualities, that is, greater than our nature. We may have a kindly nature, a philanthropic nature, or a peaceful one, but that is not we ourselves: we are greater than these.

### Releasing Concepts of God

God is far greater than what we can ever know of his nature. In order to be known, God has to be experienced, and while we can experience God through an awareness of his nature, he cannot be known with the mind or the intellect. The fact that we may have prayed to God, asking for something, is proof positive that we do not know the nature of God, for if we knew his nature, we would know that God is not withholding anything from us. God is never withholding anything from anybody on the face of the earth. How could there be a God sitting around somewhere holding on to something, withholding, or withdrawing something?

This is as impossible to believe as it would be to imagine the sun being displeased with us some day and saying, "I am going to give you light today, but no warmth," or "I will give you warmth today, but no light." How ridiculous it would be for us to pray, "O God, make the sun give us light today; make the sun give us warmth today."

But that is no more ridiculous than for us to pray to God for any other thing because when we do, we are saying in effect, "Come, God, you are withholding something I need, something you know I need, and something I must have. Give it to me!" That is like a child begging his mother for the candy that is not good for him, even though the child, of course, thinks it is.

When we know the nature of God, we become relaxed in our whole mind and body, never making a mental effort to reach out to God for anything, and never becoming tense waiting for him to give us something. We will never think in terms of a demonstration to be made in the future because there are no demonstrations in the future: there is only living in this eternal moment in which we are life itself, and we are living that life, living the life that is God—unlimited, infinite, eternal, and immortal life.

The moment we begin to know the nature of God, we find life eternal, and we are no longer wasting our life away looking to God for something that we already are, and eternally have. A weight drops from our shoulders as we realize, "I do not have to get; I do not have to wait or pray for anything; I do not have to earn or deserve it."

We may have sacrificed, hoping thus to please God, or we may have done something else with that same objective in mind; but the truth is that there is no way in which we could displease him, we who are his image and likeness, God itself in expression.

## *Breaking Karmic Law*

How can we love the God we have created in our mind, the punishing God, the rewarding God, the God that makes us wait for our good, the God that holds us in condemnation for the very sins that we could not help committing when, according to the commonly accepted concept of God, he gave us the power to do the sinning?

God is of "purer eyes than to behold evil."[1] God never holds us in bondage to our errors, and if we wish to understand the nature of punishment, we must seek for that understanding in a different direction, for God knows nothing about it. Punishment which is the inevitable consequence of wrongdoing of any sort, even that which is ignorantly done, is the reflex action of the sin itself.

There is sin which results in punishment, and there is punishment which is a consequence of sin, but they are always together, two ends of the same stick. There is no way to sin and to escape punishment because they are one, just as the consequence of sticking one's hand into an electric fan would inevitably be the loss of, or serious injury to, one's fingers. There would be no point in blaming the fan: it is not punishing the person in any way. So also there is no use blaming God. God is not inflicting any punishment. Losing or injuring the fingers is just the end result of sticking the hand into the fan. Whatever we set in motion has a reverse action. Whatever of good we do returns good to us; whatever of evil or wrong we do, also, returns in that form to us.

When we realize, however, that we of ourselves are doing neither the good nor the evil, we break the karmic law. Then, we are a transparency, an instrument, through which God's goodness flows.

We have no good *of our own.* There is no wealth of our own: there is only the wealth of God, the substance of God which is ours to share. There is no wisdom of our own: all wisdom is of God, and it is our privilege and joy to share it. There is no love that we can keep locked up within ourselves that belongs to us: love is of God, and therefore, we can release the love within us, and in doing this, we overcome the karma of sin and of punishment.

When we realize that we are but the transparency through which God flows, the instrument for God's good to reach mankind, the instrument for blessing our home, family, friends, practice, student body, and the world, when we realize that we are but a point in consciousness through which God's grace is permitted to flow to bless those receptive and responsive to it, we then have no responsibility for being good and we have no possibility of being bad.

True, there will be little human faults that will remain with all of us because we are still part and parcel of that ancient Adamic belief in two powers, but to the degree that we realize, "I can do neither good nor evil: I am but the transparency through which God appears; I am the instrument through which God's grace is flowing," then we have no qualities of good or of evil, and then we have neither good karma nor bad karma. We are just the spiritual offspring of God, eternally being the Son of God, and that is being neither good nor evil: that is being perfect.

## *The Spiritual Life, an Act of Grace*

As we come to know God, an inner sense of relaxation and peace comes in the realization, "Thank you, Father; all that you are, I am; all that you have is mine." There is no future about that—there is not even a past about it.

That is the attainment of the mind that was also in Christ Jesus. It is brought about primarily through our own efforts with, of course, the understanding that we could not be making this effort but for the grace of God. It is well to remember that we have no choice as to whether we shall follow a spiritual path and live the spiritual life, or whether we shall not follow it. If mankind had any such choice, everyone would be on the spiritual path because the fruitage is so worthwhile.

There is no way other than the spiritual path to attain lasting harmony, peace, quiet, inner joy, and prosperity. Nobody has ever attained these merely by the acquisition of health, wealth, or fame, but nobody has ever lost his inner peace and joy who has found them on the spiritual path. It is safe to say, therefore, that since everyone is seeking safety, security, peace, prosperity, and health, and since these are the concomitants of the spiritual life, many more people would be on this path than now are if they had a choice. But it is not possible for anyone to choose this life.

We come to the spiritual life by an act of grace. For example, no one is reading this book by virtue of his own will: it is because of a propulsion, a direction, or a leading that has come from a source greater than the individual himself. If the millions of other people in the world were asked to devote an hour or so to such reading, most of them would be busy with something legitimate that would make it impossible for them to do that.

There are a few who devote hours to this purpose because there is within them a something carrying them further and further along the spiritual path. As they move along on the path, they go from one stage of consciousness to another, each stage evidencing the degree of unfoldment that has taken place, and the extent to which they are going forward.

### Extending Our Horizons

When a person reaches the point where he comes to spiritual teaching for help, usually he will put forth considerable effort and devotion, spending both time and money; but all this effort, devotion, time, and money are being spent for the furthering of his own spiritual progress. In this first stage, he is not thinking in terms of a spiritual way of life; he is not thinking in terms of a world struggling for freedom: he is seeking primarily for something that will meet his own individual needs and, surprisingly enough, sometimes he will not make too much effort, or spend too much money, even in seeking his own welfare. The time does come, even in these first years, however, when he will go to any amount of trouble, give any amount of devotion, or spend any amount of money for the purpose of meeting his needs.

When the student arrives at the second stage, he has already received some measure of healing and harmony, and is beginning to think in terms of others. He tries to interest his friends and relatives in the teaching he has found; he buys books to give them, or in some other way gives something of himself to, and for, others. When that happens, we can be assured that he has entered the path and that he will undoubtedly go deeper and deeper into spiritual consciousness because he is now thinking less in terms of himself, less of his own progress, less of his personal welfare, and is beginning to share and include others in his concern.

As the entire emphasis shifts from himself to others, however, he is no longer concerned about what he can get from the teaching, or whether it will give him all that he needs. By this time, enough fruitage has appeared in his experience so that it is virtually taken for granted that this is his way. With this attitude, he has entered the third stage, which is an essential stage before he can come into the fullness of spiritual consciousness and experience the fruitage of the added things. This is the place in consciousness where he is beginning to think in terms of the particular message and of how it can help the world. Now his thought centers on how he can give of himself, how he can serve in some way so that others may find benefit from this work, how can he devote himself unselfishly to a spiritual work. There is now not a seeking to draw to himself, but rather a seeking to give of himself, to devote himself to others, a seeking to benefit the world. Rather than permitting his life to be centered in his own welfare and that of his family, his horizon is now being broadened to embrace the whole world.

Universal consciousness is being tapped, and the state the Master described as loving our neighbor as ourselves is being achieved—not at a single bound because it is impossible for a *human being* to love his neighbor as fully and completely as himself. A human being loves himself first, and his family second, but rarely, if ever, does a human being's thought go beyond himself and his family. Sometimes social pressure compels him to support the Red Cross, the Y.M.C.A., the Boy Scouts, or some other community project, but usually this is done more or less reluctantly, and not to the full measure of his financial ability.

Because humanhood is bound up entirely in its own welfare and the welfare of what it considers its own family—parents, husband, wife, child, sisters, or brothers—if a person's concern goes much further than that, it is certain that he is beginning to break through, and expand out of, his humanhood. It is only as the boundaries of humanhood are broken that a person becomes aware that there are families across the tracks whose children do not have the opportunity for a summer holiday, or who do not have adequate clothing or schooling, and then he begins to be more public-spirited. It is not really being public-spirited at all: he is but breaking through the bonds of humanhood into that spiritual state of consciousness which loves its neighbor as itself.

In the human scene, the struggle for existence is intense: the struggle to make an adequate livelihood, to meet one's bills on time and still have a little left over, or to keep one's business solvent. This is characteristic of that limited human consciousness that can feed only upon itself, relying on its own physical strength, education, personal experience, or the influence that can be brought to bear upon the situation. This is all part of the limitation of humanhood.

To those on the spiritual path, there comes a period when this struggle lessens: life becomes more fruitful and labor less arduous. Usually, this period coincides with that second stage of development when we are beginning to think of others and of sharing with them, when we are beginning to see that there are others who have problems in the world and that, perhaps, as neighbors, we can do something about them. As we begin to concern ourselves less with personal problems and extend our awareness so as to embrace and include more of our neighbors, we find that our business pressures decrease, our income increases, our worries lessen, and our fears begin to be dispelled.

We now have less concern about our own demonstration—primarily because we are being taken care of better than ever before. We are beginning to comprehend and apply the idea of loving our neighbor, with an expanding concept of neighbor which may reach out to those in other countries, and which encompasses the idea of giving, of service, of devotion to others, and in some way of helping to improve the world atmosphere and the lot of mankind through an activity of consciousness which takes the form of very human and concrete ways of service. Love is not an abstraction; love is more than piously saying, "God is love." Love must be implemented by deeds, not words.

It is in this third stage that we notice the miracle that has taken place in our life: life has ceased to be a struggle, and the "added things" come pouring in upon us, not by "taking thought," not by "demonstrating" them, but as the reflex action of the givingness of ourselves.

## The Principle of Outpouring

There are some branches of metaphysics that teach that it is possible to demonstrate supply, and that if certain prayers or treatments are repeated frequently and vigorously enough they will increase supply whether it be a supply of money, of business, or of opportunity. This approach has often failed to produce the desired results, and the hoped-for supply has usually eluded those seeking after it.

The major reason for this failure is that supply is not to be found in this world—not for you and not for me. There is no supply out here at all. All supply is embodied within our consciousness; it is omnipresent in our consciousness. Supply is infinite. We can never increase it; it is already all that the Father has.

The only bread that we can have, and the only bread that will come back to us, is the bread that we cast on the waters. What we do not give out cannot come back. What we do give out cannot fail to return to us: it is earmarked for us, and no one can touch it without burning his fingers.

We are not finite human beings: we are the life of God in individual expression, embodying everything necessary for our experience. It is much like an individual seed. It contains within itself everything necessary for its unfoldment and development into a full-grown tree with fruit on it. The tiny seed, by virtue of an activity within itself, draws unto itself from its surroundings its particular needs without taking anything from the tree or the plant next to it.

So with us. Our good appears to come to us through outside activities—a business, a profession, or through some other person—but even though we seem to be drawing our supply from these sources, nevertheless it cannot come to us unless we set in motion the activity of consciousness within ourselves that draws back unto us that which is already our own.

In this third stage of spiritual unfoldment, we learn that our participation in a spiritual activity and our desire to contribute to the betterment of mankind and to be active in some service that is to benefit others are the putting out of the bread that is to return to us. This is the truth which every mystic has known: the secret is giving, not getting; outpouring, not withholding; selflessness, not selfishness. It is only in proportion to the outpouring of ourselves, to our dedication and service to others, and to what we give that the return can come to us.

## *The Principle of Tithing*

In biblical days, this lesson was taught to the Hebrews in the form of tithing, and there are some religious movements today that still operate from the standpoint of tithing. Those persons who understand what they are doing when they tithe benefit tremendously and experience the infinite and abundant nature of their supply. Others tithe and receive no benefit because they do not understand the significance and implications of tithing.

When a person tithes with the expectation of a return, he has lost the entire benefit of tithing, and not only is there no return, but he no longer has what he has given. When a person believes that he should receive some return for his service and devotion to his particular spiritual or religious activity, he has lost any benefit that might possibly accrue to him. It is only when the giving, service, and devotion are an outpouring of his love and of his desire that others may benefit from it that it becomes a law of supply to him.

This is why it is difficult and well-nigh impossible to teach the law of supply to our friends, relatives, or students, until such time as they give evidence that they have discovered it for themselves. Otherwise, the teaching of this law is likely to set them on the wrong path and leave them with the impression that if only they give there will be a return to them. There is no return as a result of giving except when the giving is the spontaneous love that flows out from a person, compelling him to do what he is doing.

It is that same inner compulsion that must operate in bringing a person to a spiritual message; he must always be led from within his own being. True, it is a loving and generous thing to give or send someone a pamphlet, a book, or something that may show him that there is another way of life than the one he now knows. But rarely is it wisdom to go further than that, for the simple reason that until the person himself responds, the spiritual life is not for him. There are some who are ready for this kind of life, but there are many others who are not ready, and each one must be permitted to go his own way in complete freedom.

When we come into contact with others, we must be careful not to attempt to force anyone into accepting our way of life, into giving, sharing, or serving in any form, but rather let the unfoldment come forth from within the person himself. Only when we witness that it is taking place, can we know that our friend, relative, or student is now on the spiritual path and on the threshold of demonstrating that all that the Father has is his—allness embodied within him.

## The Infinite and Omnipresent Nature of Supply

There is enough good in this world to supply everyone who is now living on the earth, and all those who are to come. Everybody could be living in infinite abundance with what is in, on, and above the earth today—and what is not there, God has provided us with means to get.

There is enough in this world to give us all an infinity of supply if only we are willing to share it, if only we are willing to let it pour forth. Supply is giving, sharing, outpouring, and that results in its incoming. But it cannot begin until we acknowledge that God has nothing left to give us, that God has implanted in our consciousness the fullness of the Godhead bodily, and now we must turn within and draw it forth, let it flow.

If we want to compose music, we turn within and find what we are seeking within our own consciousness. If we are working in the field of inventions, we do not beseech God to reveal them to us: we turn within and find that God has already planted every necessary idea within us, within our own mind and Soul and consciousness, and we need only draw forth that which is already there—give it, share it, produce it. Infinity itself is within us: eternality, immortality, an abundance of all good.

There are those who are still trying to demonstrate companionship. They will never succeed because companionship is something that is locked up within themselves, and they will never find a companion until they open out a way to express companionship. Unless they are expressing companionship, who wants them? What have they to offer? What are they offering? To get something? That is not much of an offer.

When we go out into the world with the idea of giving and sharing, we will soon discover that we have as much companionship within us as God has. The first way to begin to express it is to begin companioning with God, and as we begin to companion with God within ourselves, we find an infinity of companions on the outer plane, but until we have made our contact with the Father within, we do not make our contact with our rightful companions without.

Let us open our eyes that we may discover the infinite nature of what God has stored up in us and then open out a way for it to flow forth into expression. Whatever we seem to lack is already present in abundant measure: we merely lack the ability to let it flow out from us. What we must do is to find a way to let it flow: to give, to share, to express.

When we do this from the standpoint that we are not giving anything of our own, but that we are giving out of the infinite nature of God, the cruse of oil will never run dry. When we understand that we have nothing of ourselves, we will never lack money, companions, home, or harmony. If we had a million dollars and began giving it out, we still would not be giving anything that belonged to us. We are merely the temporary holders of it, the temporary possessors, the temporary trustees. When we give and share, let us be very certain that we know that all we are doing is being a transfer agent for the infinite source, for the cruse of oil pouring itself through us, that cruse that never runs dry.

Because God expresses as individual you and me, good must express individually as your good and mine. Since God is infinite, our good has to be infinite, and there is no room for anything less than infinite good, infinite abundance, infinite harmony, infinite life, infinite truth, and infinite love. But all this can come only as we understand that God is not withholding, that God cannot be bribed by sacrifices, and that he cannot be influenced. Not all our tears, nor all our prayers are going to influence God, any more than they would influence the sun to give us more light or more warmth, or less light or less warmth. Whatever the sun is, it is.

God is. God is; and God is now. God is the same yesterday, today, and forever. There is no way of changing God, and there is no way of changing God's plan, but we can bring ourselves into harmony as the Sons of God by the realization: "I can of my own self do nothing. I of my own self am nothing. 'Why callest thou me good? there is none good but one, that is God.'[2]" Then let us be willing that God's grace flow through us to our faraway neighbor as well as our nearby neighbor.

Let us relax in the *is-ness* of God, in the omnipresence of God, relax from praying for things, relax from striving, and live in the conscious awareness that the nature of God is infinite intelligence: it knows the need, not only of mankind, but of every insect and every blade of grass. The nature of God is infinite wisdom, and we do not tell God anything: we relax in the realization of his wisdom. The nature of God is love, and it is God's good pleasure to give us the kingdom, just as it is his good pleasure to give us light. We do not make that kingdom any more than we make light. We do not force light: we *let* there be light! We *let* God's grace function for us, *let* his will be done in earth as it is in heaven, not by might, not by power, but by his own spirit, by his own wisdom, by his own love. We relax and *let*.

## Across the Desk

In my mail from different parts of the world frequently comes the same complaint: "I am not making satisfactory spiritual progress." If these persons rightly understood The Infinite Way, such a thought would never have come into their minds. To begin with, human beings never become spiritual, so there is no such thing as making progress. The goal, if we can put it that way, is "dying daily," and the only spiritual progress they could make would be to die to their human self, their ego and all their material desires, and few there are who want to do that. They all want to make progress in getting spiritual, and this is impossible.

No human being has ever been spiritual, and no human being is ever going to be spiritual. If we want our spirituality to come to light, we have to die. The very humanhood that we want to make spiritual has to die. Dying is not an easy process, even philosophically or mystically; but it is a process, and in that process we are not going to feel that we are becoming spiritual. As a matter of fact, if we should attain spirituality, we would not feel spiritual. In my experience, at least, there has been no feeling of spirituality, and I have spoken to others who have gone far on the path, and they do not seem to know what it means to feel spiritual.

The point that we must bear in mind is not whether we are making progress. The mystical revelation is that *I* already am—*I* am not going to be. The mystical revelation is that, whereas we thought we were human, we are now learning that we are divine; whereas we thought we had a life of our own, we are now learning that God is our life; whereas we believed that we had a mind of our own, now we are discovering that our mental capacity is infinite. No process of education is going to make us spiritual or immortal. No matter what our I. Q. may be, it is not the measure of our capacity. The truth is that there is no limit to our intelligence. There may be a limit to what you and I are bringing through at any particular moment, but that limitation changes with the recognition that we have no mind of our own, that God constitutes our mind.

In the same way, many who have been brought up with some kind of church background have been taught about sin and all the things that are wrong for them to do, and some of them probably have been guilty of ninety per cent of them— if not in action, then in thought. Therefore, most people with a church background have a guilt complex and are convinced that they are not worthy of God's grace or God's love, or that they are not worthy of being saved or being healed. This is nonsense.

If Christ Jesus himself could say, "Why callest thou me good?" how can anyone rightly claim to be good? If there is any goodness manifesting through us, any integrity or morality, it is a quality of God, not of us. If we are bringing through goodness or great mental and intellectual capacity, we must die daily to the belief that we are good, that we are deserving, or that we are intelligent, die daily and acknowledge that it is only the life of God, the wisdom of God, and the love of God that are flowing through us. Then we will have "nothingized" ourselves. We will have died, and our spiritual capacity will shine through.

All this trying to be good defeats our purpose. We will be good only when we have given up being good and let God be good through us. We will never be spiritual until we have given up trying to be spiritual and recognize that God is spirit and the only spirituality about us is God. Then, this false sense of self will begin to drop away. Ours is the Father's work, and we are but instruments. "If I bear witness of myself, my witness is not true.[3] ... The Father that dwelleth in me, he doeth the works."[4] The Master recognized himself to be but an instrument through which God was functioning. This is not only humility; it is the kind of humility that permits the ego to "die" to its personal selfhood.

Throughout the writings, you will find stated over and over again that there is only one reason for our discords—physical, mental, moral, or financial—and that is the sense of separation from God, a sense of a selfhood and a life apart from God. This sense of separation is perpetuated in the degree that we are trying to improve that self instead of realizing that God's Self is already ours, and then relaxing and letting it come into manifestation. It may not come all in a moment. It may take months, sometimes years, because there is a part of us that cannot quite accept the truth that God is our Self.

This unwillingness to accept God as our Self has been the basis of all religious persecution. One of the reasons Jesus was persecuted was because he made himself equal with God. In other words, he denied himself and permitted God to be his life, his mind, his goodness, and his healing power. He claimed no healing power of his own; he claimed no saving power of his own: always it was the Father within him that did the works.

If anyone says this—and of course no one has any right to say it except in teaching—there are always those either hearing or reading it who are ready to misinterpret what has been said or written. Some years ago, a metaphysical teacher sent out letters to his students warning them not to read Joel Goldsmith's books because Mr. Goldsmith says that he is God. As you well know, I do not say that at all. I say, "*I* am God," and that is quite different because there is only one *I*, and if *I* am God, you have the same right to that *I* because nobody can patent or copyright it.

Without the revelation of *I AM THAT I AM* which Moses received, he never could have led the Hebrews away from Pharaoh, nor out through the desert, almost to freedom. If the Master had not discovered that *I* is God, his teaching would not have lasted two thousand years. His teaching of the Christ is now growing faster than at any other time in history, and all because he discovered the truth that I AM is God.

Whenever we find a teaching that has lasted two thousand or more years, we can be sure that behind it is the revelation that there is only one God, that that God was not born, did not die, and did not rise again at some particular time. God is from everlasting to everlasting. God changes not. God is infinity, omnipotence, omnipresence, omniscience, and none of that is floating around in the air. All of that is revealed as our own spiritual identity, God revealing, manifesting, and expressing himself as individual being.

You are that individual being, and if you have not yet come to a mystical teaching and do not know this, you are still searching for God, for truth. Why do you think the Master remained silent when Pilate asked him, "What is truth?" Do you think he could have answered, "I am the truth?" He could no more have done that than you could answer, "I am God," if a traffic officer stopped you and asked, "What is your name?" He might well say, "You're too old to be driving!"

We must be very careful to whom we reveal our true identity. We do not go out and say, "I am as brilliant as God," or "I am as young as God," or "I am as intelligent as God." Those are things that we reveal only to one another and, then, only to those who seek us. That is why we do not advertise our work and expect great crowds to come to our lectures. You know what would happen if I should say to them, "Stop trying to be spiritual: you are already spirit." So we do not walk up and down the world telling what we know. We keep a finger on our lips and tell this only to those who have been led to us.

Before my public work began, I was given my inner instruction, "Never seek a student"—and I never have consciously. For this reason, what I have to say is often shocking to the human mind. You will begin to appreciate how good your health is and how abundant your supply is, only when you stop trying, when you stop struggling, when you relax and rest in the assurance of your oneness with the Father. Why struggle anymore? Relax and let that unfoldment come from within.

When you realize that God constitutes individual being—God is the life of you, the mind and the Soul of you, and even your body is the temple of God—what more is there to know? You have planted the seed of truth. Now go about your business and let this seed take root. Let it manifest itself. But if you are going to fret and concern yourself and look in the mirror to see how spiritual you are becoming, you are going to miss the way. Or if you think there is some sign that is going to show you that you are more spiritual, you will miss the way. There are no signs. There is no more possibility of feeling spiritual than there is of feeling honest or of feeling moral. You *are* it, but you surely cannot feel it. If you could feel it, it would mean that there was an opposite there, some bad part of you that is admiring some good.

Let us not be concerned with spiritual progress. What you must concern yourself with is knowing the truth, the truth which will make you free from your and reveal your spiritual identity which always was, is now, and will forever be.

# * 12 *

## THE PRINCE OF PEACE

THE FULL SIGNIFICANCE of Christmas can never be known except through an understanding of the unchanging nature of God, the God who is eternally and everlastingly the same yesterday, today, and forever. That which is of God always has been, that which has been is now, and that which is now always will be. To understand this reveals that the real Christmas did not begin two thousand years ago: it began in the beginning, before time was. What took place two thousand years ago was merely the revelation of an experience that has been continuous, not only since "before Abraham was,"[1] but since before time was. God did not inaugurate anything new two thousand years ago.

The true meaning of Christmas is that God planted in individual consciousness the seed that was to evolve as his Son. No one has ever existed, exists now, or ever will exist without this spiritual influence and power having been implanted in his consciousness from the beginning.

The function of the Son of God was made clear through the ministry of Jesus Christ when he revealed, "I am come that they might have life, and that they might have it more abundantly"[2]—not I, Jesus, but I, the Son of God. Jesus said, "If I bear witness of myself, my witness is not true... . I of mine own self do nothing ...[3] I am the bread of life ...[4] I am the resurrection, and the life."[5] That was the Son of God speaking. Jesus was not all this: it was the Son of God speaking through him—the same Son of God which is

185

in the midst of all of us as it has been in the midst of every individual since the beginning of time.

### *Go Within to Find the Peace Established from the Beginning*

There is a story which tells of an ancient king who himself was peaceful, just, merciful, and kind, but who had a neighbor-king intent on war and conquest. Because of the nature of his being, the just and merciful king sent an ambassador to the neighboring king to seek peace. Meanwhile, to protect his people, he began to get ready for war, and from one end of the nation to the other, preparations were made for the expected conflict. Joy, then, went out of the hearts of the people, and smiles faded from their faces.

The king kept praying for some means of bringing about peace and harmony, and one day the wife of an official of the court came to him and asked permission to reveal a secret to him. What she whispered in his ear made him smile, and he told her to go out and seek out other women in the city— not the men, just the women—confide to each woman this secret, and let news of it go throughout the city and the land. The king then went to his own wife, told her what he had learned, and she, also, went abroad in the land and imparted this great secret to all the women she met. So, from end to end of this nation, as the women traveled and whispered their message to one another, smiles began to return to the faces of the people, singing was heard in the land again, and joy was abroad.

On Christmas Day, word came from the ambassador to the neighboring country that a peace treaty had been signed. When the king then issued an edict that all war preparations were to cease and that the people were to turn to the making of peaceful goods, he learned that this had already been done, and that this was part of the reason for the merriment in the land. Then, of course, all the officials of the court wanted to know what had produced this miraculous change. The king explained that the secret one woman had whispered to another was: "Every day retire for a short period of silence. Go within and pray to God, but do not pray to God for peace. Do not pray to God for anything at all. Just sit in the silence and find peace within yourself; feel peace within yourself; and do this every day." This was the great secret of joy and merriment again, and of peace with the neighboring country.

To Infinite Way students, this is not a strange story because we have long realized that we cannot pray to God for peace in the nation, or even peace for ourselves. God has planted peace in our Souls, in our hearts, and in our minds. As human beings, it lies buried there, and to resurrect it, we must go within and meet the peace that is there before this peace can become "the imprisoned splendour" that escapes out into the world for our neighbors to feel.

The function of that Son of God is that we may have peace, that we may have life more abundant, and that we may find within ourselves all that the Father has. "Son, thou art ever with me, and all that I have is thine,"[6] and this *all* is planted within us. When we dig oil wells, when we mine for gold, silver, or diamonds, when we dive for pearls, are we not bringing forth that which God has already planted in the midst of us? Are we responsible for all that is in the soil, all that is in the ocean, and all that is in the air? Have we created this good in the earth, above the earth, and beneath the earth, or has all this been placed here for our benefit? Of course, the answer is that all these riches in the earth have been forming for millions upon millions of years, long before there were any people to have need of them. All we have to do is to bring forth that which God has planted in the midst of us.

This is true also of the spiritual universe. The kingdom of God is not "Lo here! or Lo there! for, behold, the kingdom of God is within you."[7] How, then, are we to enjoy this kingdom except by finding it within ourselves, except by making contact with it, except by digging and diving, and the deeper we dig and the deeper we dive into that inner silence, the greater the treasure we bring forth.

### Our Individual Life
### must Show Forth God's Grace

To understand Christmas Day, then, let us understand clearly that God has planted the seed of himself in each of us, the seed that springs forth as the fully developed Son of God whose mission it is that our lives may be fulfilled, that we may show forth the glory of God which the Master revealed. Since "I can of mine own self do nothing," since "if I bear witness of myself, my witness is not true,"[8] then all that we must do with our individual lives is to show forth God's grace: his wisdom, spirit, health, and abundance. This must be both the possibility and the potentiality of every individual. Otherwise, it could not truthfully be said that God is from everlasting to everlasting, that God is the same, and that God is no respecter of persons.

If what God has done is forever, then, since the beginning of time, mankind has had within its own Soul the divine peace and the divine grace of God. Unfortunately, we cannot give that to our neighbors, nor can we receive it from our neighbors until we have found it within ourselves. What we do not have, we cannot give. Jesus said, "For unto whomsoever much is given, of him shall be much required."[9] So it is to be expected that those who find peace within themselves will bestow this peace upon their neighbors.

If we have not found the Christ within ourselves, however, we cannot share the Christ with another. If we do not feel peace toward our neighbors, we have no peace to share with them, and we cannot bring forth peace from our neighbors. No one who is not expressing love can draw love to himself; no one who is not expressing abundance can draw abundance to himself; no one who has not found peace within himself can draw peace to himself. Whatever it is that we would share with our family, community, or with the world at large must first be found within ourselves.

Even Jesus had nothing to give the world until the Christ had been revealed in him. "The Spirit of the Lord God is upon me, because he hath anointed me to preach the gospel to the poor; he hath sent me to heal the broken-hearted, to preach deliverance to the captives, and recovering of sight to the blind."[10] Until that ordination, he was not anointed to heal the sick; and before anyone can share the spirit of peace, joy, love, and abundance, he must first be ordained with the spirit of God.

### Peace Has to Begin with Us

Christmas would be of little value to us and have no significance if we believed that the Prince of Peace lived two thousand years ago but is not on earth today. True, the Prince of Peace did live two thousand years ago, and four thousand years ago, too, just as the Prince of Peace is also on earth today in the heart, the Soul, and in the consciousness of every individual awaiting to be released into this world.

This Christ-peace, however, cannot be achieved by praying to God to reform our neighbors—not even our neighbors across the sea! It has to begin with us.

Why do we not recognize our own barrenness before we begin to demand things of others? Let us leave our neighbors alone, and secretly and sacredly go within, silently communing with the Prince of Peace within us, the Prince of joy, health, wholeness, completeness, and of spiritual perfection. Then, when we have attained some measure of Christhood and are no longer barren, we will not have to ask for peace from our neighbor, nor will we have to pray to God for peace, for peace will be flowing out from within ourselves to all mankind.

The peace that passes understanding is established within us, and it is given release when we make contact with it in our daily meditations. Like a dove, it begins to spread its wings over this entire universe. To look for peace in another is not only to evade and avoid the issue: it is to prevent our own experience of peace. To look for justice, for mercy, or for gratitude in another is a mistake. It is our individual responsibility to find the kingdom of God at the center of our own being.

When the Master spoke to the people on the shores of Galilee, wherever two or more could be gathered together—in the mountains, by the lakes, in the desert, and in the wilderness—he always used the word "you." *You* must forgive seventy times seven; *you* must pray for your enemy; *you* must seek first the kingdom of God that is within *you*. Always, he was speaking to those who would listen to him. He did not say these things to Pilate or to Herod; he did not say them to Caesar; he did not look to them for peace. He looked to the *"you's"* before him, knowing that if they found peace within themselves, that peace would envelop all mankind.

So it is that when we begin to take the responsibility for maintaining the health and the harmony of our own families, we discover that the inner peace and harmony we find in our moments of meditation become the law of health and harmony to our children and to other members of our family. Later, as we accept the responsibility of helping our neighbors or our friends and relatives who ask for help, we do not tell them to be healthy, wealthy, just, or merciful. We retire to that secret place within ourselves, and there commune with this Son of God until the feeling of peace envelops us; and when we find our peace, those who have come to us for help also receive their peace. We have not transferred it to them by any mental abracadabra, or by suggestion or hypnotism: we have turned to the kingdom of God within, and there found peace, oneness, and spiritual communion with the Christ, and then this influence escapes from us and becomes a law of life and of love to those who look to us for help.

One of the very earliest revelations given to me was that it is not necessary for me to pray for anyone or to give treatments to anyone: it is only necessary for me to find my own inner peace, and then the peace that I find, the awareness of harmony, wholeness, completeness, immediately becomes the experience of those turning to me for help. They have attuned themselves to my consciousness in the same way that the woman who pressed through the throng and touched the hem of Jesus' robe attuned herself to his Christ-consciousness, and then the peace that enveloped him descended upon her, and she was healed.

## The Dignity and Sacredness of the Individual

The significance of the Christ is lost if we do not understand that the healing Christ was never crucified and was never buried in a tomb. The healing Christ is the Prince of Peace within us, the Son of God planted there from the beginning. Through our meditations, through an inner contemplation and communion with that spirit within, we raise up this Son in us, and that communion brings forth in our universe all that the Son of God is.

It is a miracle of grace that where only two or more are gathered together in his name, there they find the entire kingdom of God in the midst of them. It is a miracle of grace that one with God is a majority. Every single life is a miracle of God's grace; every individual is an offspring of the most High.

The Western World must learn to appreciate the dignity of individual man before it will have the full moral force that will eventually bring peace on earth. Peace will not be established by military means: peace will be established by the moral capacity of those nations that have grasped the significance of the value of an individual, and the reason for that value. As a human being, an individual is not valuable. It is because God has incarnated himself as man and because every individual potentially is the Christ, the Prince of Peace, that he is as important to God as the greatest of the prophets, saints, and saviors.

If only ten righteous men could realize the dignity and sacredness of individual man, they would act with such moral force as to change the nature of the affairs of a whole city, state, or nation, and eventually this realization would govern international relationships. There must, however, be this lifting up of the Christ-ideal of the nature of individual being; there must be the recognition of ourselves as the offspring of God; there must be the conviction that our life is not really ours, but the life of God individually expressed through us as you and as me, the mind of God individually manifested as your mind and mine.

If all we are is what we see in our mirrors, what is the reason for our existence on earth? If we examine the lives of some human beings, we must wonder why they are even tolerated in this world of ours. Only when we begin to understand the nature of this that is inherent in us and that this now awaits raising up in us for our redemption, for our functioning as children of God on earth, only then do we realize that we are sent to show forth all of God's glory. This is the true Christmas; this is the Christ-mass.

"For I came down from heaven not to do mine own will, but the will of him that sent me,"[11] So says the Master, and because of the universal nature of God, it is your function and mine to live so that God's will may be done through us, not your will and not mine. Our lives must be dedicated to that principle. Wherever there is an individual capable of putting himself aside and realizing, "I am here that God's will may be done through me; I am here so as to be an outlet for this 'imprisoned splendour'; I am here that I may be used so that this Christ within may function for the benefit of all those who are still in darkness," there the Christ abides and lives that life.

It was Napoleon who said that every soldier has a marshal's baton in his knapsack, and this is merely another way of expressing the Christ-teaching that every man, by the grace of God's presence in him, has within himself the full authority and dignity of a master.

The world has been fortunate in having had great teachers who caught the vision of the indwelling spirit of God and who realized the divine nature of man: Moses, Elijah, Elisha, Isaiah, Jesus, John, and Paul, Buddha, Shankara, and Nanak. All these men taught the same thing—that they were only way-showers, teachers, and that if they did not go away, the Comforter could not come. If we, too, do not begin to perceive that what has been revealed by the spiritual masters of the world is a universal principle, how, then, can this Christ become a universal revelation and demonstration? How can the kingdom of God come on earth if it does not come as individual man raised up to his Christhood?

Are the people of this world of themselves suddenly going to become good people instead of bad people, wise people instead of ignorant people? Is there anything that is going to change the human race from being what it always has been—a state of slavery, a state of bondage, a state of mass ignorance? Will the world ever change except through the realization of the nature of Christmas, the nature of the truth that the seed of God is planted in human consciousness, planted in individual you and me, and that we must bring forth our spiritual identity? Is there any other way in which it can be done?

Education, of course, is a valuable adjunct to a civilized society, but mere academic training and intellectual prowess do not bring forth morality or integrity. Only the realization of the spiritual nature of our being can do that, only the lifting up of the Christ in us can make us a world of people inspired with high spiritual and moral sense, and this by releasing it from within ourselves. Telling people that they should be good, that there should be peace on earth, or that there should be integrity in their dealings with others does not bring it about. Nothing does—not even preaching sermons. Only in one way can peace be established on earth, and that is to find the peace of God in our own being. As we do that, we will attract to ourselves little groups, and they will find the peace of God established within them. Then they, in turn, finding the peace of God within themselves, will draw it forth from others, and so on *ad infinitum*.

## *Releasing the "Imprisoned Splendour"*

Peace is locked up in you and in me, and we must release the Prince of Peace from within us, and then let it do its work in the consciousness of all those who at this moment may be ready and receptive for the experience. This is not done by moralizing to the world or by asking the world to be better than it is, or is capable of being. It is done individually by releasing that Prince of Peace within ourselves, by communing with the spirit within, and then, as it escapes, letting it go before us to do its work. We are not called upon to go out into the world-only to release the spirit of Christ into the world.

There is no spiritual value in all the thousands of words that we utter. There is no spiritual or moral value in all the hundreds of lessons we teach or preach. The grace of God does not reach human consciousness by moralizing. What we must do is to retire to our homes, to our temples, to our hills and valleys, and there find the peace hidden within. We must become centers through which the grace of God can escape, and then that invisible presence goes before us to make the crooked places straight and to prepare mansions for us. Our greatest value to the world lies in our periods of silence, secrecy, and sacredness.

Every time that we see a person and realize that this grace of God is within him, we become a light unto the world—without voicing it, speaking, uttering, or writing it, but merely by looking on an individual and realizing that there, too, is the grace of God, there, too, is the Son of God. This is releasing the "imprisoned splendour"; this is the recognition of the indwelling Christ in friend and foe—not the recognition of a human being walking the earth, but a recognition of the seed planted in the midst of him.

This seed that lies buried within us will remain a seed forever until it receives its nourishment, and that spiritual nourishment so necessary is the recognition of the true identity of the individual:

*Within individual man is the Son of God, that I that he is. Within him is the divine presence and the divine power, the grace of God. I within him, is the food, the sunshine, and the rain to that seed.*

Then the seed begins to sprout, and the nature of our friends, relatives, and business associates changes before our very eyes without their even knowing why. There may develop in them a search for God, a seeking for reality, until a message or messenger reveals that it is not necessary to seek further because it is within. That which we are seeking is the divine reality of us, the Son of God in us, the Holy Grail within our own consciousness.

All the sacredness of the Son of God is established at the center of our being—the eternality, the immortality, the infinite nature of God's being—because we are one with the Father, and all that the Father has is already ours: his wisdom, his mind, his glory, his grace, his presence, his substance, his being. The very breath of his life is the breath of our life, for we are one, and in that oneness we find our allness and our oneness with all mankind. Only in our oneness with God are we at-one with every spiritual light who has ever trod the globe—past, present, and future.

Christmas reveals that God has planted his Son in us.

## Across the Desk

All spiritual teaching is taught by means of symbols, allegories, or parables; and so it is that the story of the virgin birth goes back thousands of years before the days of the Master. In the spiritual literature of the world, there are seven spiritual leaders credited with having been born of a virgin. Jesus is not the first, he is the seventh and last. Before him there were six others, one of whom was Gautama, the Buddha.

Those who are familiar with the story of Gautama's birth will remember that when his father married a virgin, he recognized that her virginity was of such a nature that she was to bring forth for the world its savior, and he knew her not. The heavens lit up; the sun, the moon, and the stars trembled; and a great music was heard in the air. She conceived and, in due time, brought forth Gautama who later was known as the Buddha. Upon his birth, the holy men of India went to the palace to see this babe, and as one old sage and seer made his acknowledgments, he exclaimed, "I have lived only for this hour that I might see and recognize this babe."

All of this is repeated hundreds of years later in the account of the virgin birth of Jesus, of the holy men who journeyed to Bethlehem to pay homage to him, and of the Wise Men who acknowledged him. Every major religious teaching has been founded upon the idea of a virgin birth, and although what was meant was the virgin birth of the teaching, that eventually became identified as the virgin birth of the original revelator. But fundamentally it is meant to be symbolic.

The Christ is always of virgin birth because it comes to us by no human or physical process. It is the grace of God entering our consciousness; and when it does, it enters as a babe, so tiny that we are almost afraid to acknowledge that we have had a spiritual experience, afraid we may have deceived ourselves because it was of such fleeting duration that we are not even certain that we are not fooling ourselves in remembering it. It is so gentle an experience that we cannot be sure that it ever happened. Yet as we ponder, continue to think and to meditate, this Babe that has been conceived in us unfolds and lets us become aware of its presence, but always in such a way that we are not quite positive of it, and certainly we are not strong in it.

Then comes the Birth. When the Birth takes place, it brings with it such very visible and tangible effects that we know beyond all doubt that the Christ has touched us. Then, the world tries to kill it for us because the world does not want us to have this glorious thing, and it begins immediately to tell us how wrong we are and how we are deluding ourselves.

Nevertheless, when the Christ is born in us, it changes the whole nature of our life; it changes the whole nature of our character, it changes the whole nature of our immortal experience. Never again will we be called upon to live our own life, but now if we are wise, instead of telling it to others, showing it to others, or trying to prove it to others, we take it down into Egypt, the place of darkness, and there keep it hidden, letting the Christ in our experience be revealed only by its effects in our life. Why voice it or try to convince anyone? We may as well try to convince a person born blind of sunshine. How can we explain something to people who have no way of receiving it? They are not living on that level of consciousness. How can we tell a person who has not attained the consciousness able to recognize the Christ that he should live by grace, without worry, fear, accidents, death, or poverty?

So, in our wisdom, we carry the Babe down to Egypt, hide it, tell no one about it, and let others see it only by its effect until we ourselves are so strengthened in it that we arrive at that place of conviction where, if necessary, we would go to prison for it, or would allow ourselves to be thrown into a den of lions, or be crucified for it.

When this Christ takes over in our experience and begins to produce fruitage for us, the world, which does not understand and cannot believe, will do its best to take it from us, or if it cannot succeed in doing this, will attempt to destroy us. But if we are grounded, if we have come to a place of conviction where we know that there is no power that can overthrow the Christ, there is no power on earth that can undo the work of God, we no longer resort to human means. Then, we have the full and complete Christ, and it becomes our way.

The Christ-experience can come, as it has come to some persons, for no apparent human reason—just as a gift of God. It has come to some without their knowing why, without their deserving or being worthy of it. In such cases, however, they were prepared for it in a previous experience—their consciousness had been prepared, and they had undoubtedly come back into this human experience for the very purpose of attaining their Christhood in order to be spiritually equipped to perform some specific work in the world.

These gifts of God are never given to an individual as a reward for anything, or for his own personal pleasure or profit. They are never meant to glorify an individual or to set anyone up. That is why Jesus Christ refused honors during his lifetime. Always he disclaimed anything in the way of a personal message or gift; he set aside human selfhood. Always his work was to glorify God that had sent him into expression. So it is that when a gift of God is given, it is for God's purpose on earth.

As we follow the lives of all those who have been ordained of God and received the revelation leading to the founding of new religious teachings, we find that humility is their outstanding quality, not a false sense of humility that robes itself in a sanctimonious air, but a real sense of humility which comes from an absolute knowledge that whatever it is that is taking place through them is not of their own doing. It is an impulsion from an infinite source, and it does not come so that the individual will achieve fame or amass great wealth: it comes so that that individual, in forgetting self, will carry forward whatever the mission is that goes with the spiritual gift given him.

There is no Christ-experience for anyone while he is living on the human plane. There must be a purification of consciousness, a baptism of the spirit, the descent of the Holy Ghost, in which human judgment, criticism, and condemnation are lost, and we become of too pure eyes to behold iniquity. Even when we are aware of evil, we are inwardly praying, "Father, forgive them," because we understand that all evil is impersonal and has its foundation in an impersonal belief in two powers.

The state of consciousness that does not accept two powers is a consciousness that can receive the Christ because it is a pure or virgin state of consciousness. It knows neither pain nor pleasure: it knows only God, only spiritual enlightenment and spiritual joy. It does not have good health or bad health: it is a state of divine being.

When we are not a house divided against ourselves, when we are not a divided consciousness, we are pure, and the Christ can find entrance. The Christ always comes to us with the name I: "I am with you. I will never leave you. I will be with you to the end of the world. I will go before you and prepare mansions for you." It always speaks to us from the center of our being with that word I. But this can only come when we can realize that every man has the same spiritual, virgin consciousness that we have, only he may not yet be aware of it.

The birth of the Christ is the advent of divine grace in human consciousness. It cannot be explained: it is a virgin experience that takes place within us without any material accompaniment. With that experience, a new plateau is attained, and from its heights a new horizon glimpsed, beckoning us forward and onward.

# Scriptural References and Notes

## Awake

1. Isaiah 26:3
2. Proverbs 3:6
3. Isaiah 30:15
4. *The Song Celestial*,
Trans, by Sir Edwin Arnold
(Philadelphia, PA: David McKay Co.)

## 1. The Spiritual New Year

1. Galatians 5:1
2. II Corinthians 6:17
3. Isaiah 45:2
4. Matthew 5:48
5. Philippians 3:13
6. John 10:30
7. John 16:33
8. Mark 2:11
9. Matthew 12:13
10. John 10:30
11. John 14:9

## 2. The One Great Demonstration

1. John 8:32
2. John 5:30
3. Matthew 6:25, 32
4. Psalm 43:5
5. II Samuel 22:2, 3
6. II Corinthians 3:17
7. Luke 15:31
8. II Corinthians 12:9
9. Psalm 16:11
10. John 5:30; 14:10
11. John 14:10
12. Galatians 2:20
13. Matthew 4:4
14. Isaiah 2:22
15. John 14:10
16. Galatians 2:20
17. I John 4:4
18. Job 23:14
19. Psalm 138:8
20. John 12:45
21. John 10:30
22. Psalm 23:4

23. Luke 17:21      24. I Samuel 3:9

25. Psalm 46:6

## 3. THE TRUTH THAT MAKES FREE

1. Acts 10:11, 12      2. I Corinthians 2:14

3. Isaiah 30:21      4. II Chronicles 32:6, 8

5. Matthew 17:21      6. By the author

7. By the author

## 4. CHRIST RAISED FROM THE TOMB

1. John 5:30, 31      2. John 7:16

3. John 14:10      4. Psalm 46:10

5. I Corinthians 2:14      6. Romans 8:9

7. I Samuel 3:9      8. John 18:36

9. Psalm 19:1      10. Galatians 2:20

11. Luke 4:8

## 5. WITHINNESS

1. John 8:32      2. Galatians 6:7

3. Galatians 6:8      4. John 8:11

5. Ezekiel 18:32      6. Matthew 5:39

7. Luke 4:8      8. Ecclesiastes 11:1

9. Matthew 23:9      10. Luke 23:34

## 6. BRINGING GRACE INTO ACTIVE EXPRESSION

1. John 15:6      2. Romans 8:9

3. Isaiah 2:22      4. John 16:7

5. Luke 17:21      6. Isaiah 26:3

7. Isaiah 30:15      8. Psalm 121:1

### 7. The Power to Become the Son of God

1. Deuteronomy 6:4
2. Galatians 2:20
3. Romans 8:9

### 8. Rising Above "This World"

1. *The Infinite Way*, by the author
2. John 19:11
3. John 5:8
4. John 8:11
5. By the author, *op. cit.*
6. *Ibid.*
7. Isaiah 44:8
8. By the author, *op. cit.*
9. *Ibid.*
10. *Ibid.*
11. *Ibid.*
12. *Ibid.*
13. *Ibid.*
14. *Ibid.*
15. *Ibid.*
16. John 18:36
17. Hebrews 8:5
18. Philippians 2:5
19. Psalm 24:1
20. Luke 15:31
21. John 18:36

### 9. Spiritual Dominion

1. Isaiah 2:22
2. John 10:30
3. Luke 15:31
4. Hebrews 13:5
5. Matthew 28:20
6. Psalm 139:8
7. Psalm 23:4
8. John 14:6
9. John 6:35
10. John 11:25
11. Matthew 6:25
12. Isaiah 2:22
13. John 15:5
14. John 19:11
15. Psalm 24:1
16. Romans 8:8, 14
17. II Corinthians 5:17
18. John 10:30
19. John 6:38
20. John 18:36
21. Galatians 2:20

## 10. The Meaning of Prayer

1. Galatians 5:6
2. Luke 11:9
3. John 6:35
4. Matthew 6:11
5. John 6:35
6. Matthew 6:33
7. Matthew 6:19, 20
8. John 15:7
9. John 15:6
10. Isaiah 26:3
11. Luke 4:18
12. Romans 8:9
13. Psalm 23:4
14. Psalm 19:1
15. Hebrews 13:5
16. John 8:58
17. Ruth 1:16
18. Matthew 23: 9
19. Isaiah 55:8
20. Isaiah 26:3

## 11. Breaking the Bonds of Humanhood

1. Habakkuk 1:13
2. Matthew 19:17
3. John 5:31
4. John 14:10

## 12. The Prince of Peace

1. John 8:58
2. John 10:10
3. John 5:31, 30
4. John 6:35
5. John 11:25
6. Luke 15:31
7. Luke 17:21
8. John 5:30, 31
9. Luke 12:48
10. Luke 4:18
11. John 6:38

# Joel Goldsmith Recorded Classes Corresponding to the Chapters of This Book

Many of Joel Goldsmith's books, including this one, are based on his recorded classwork, which has been preserved in tape, CD, and MP3 formats by the Infinite Way Office in Moreno Valley, CA.

The listing below shows the classes related to each chapter of this book. For example, "#159-1 1956 Chicago Closed Class 2:1" means:

The recording number is 159, Side 1 **(#159-1)**.

The recording is from the **1956 Chicago Closed Class**.

The recording is Tape 2, Side 1 for the 1956 Chicago Closed Class **(2:1)**.

1. **The Spiritual New Year**
   #385-1: 1960/61 Christmas & New Year's - Waikiki 2:1

2. **The One Great Demonstration**
   #301-1: 1960 Los Angeles Closed Class 1:1

3. **The Truth That Makes Free**
   #318-2: 1960 Kansas City Practitioner Class 1:2

4. **Christ Raised from the Tomb**
   #441-2: 1961 Hawaiian Village Open Class 5:2

## 5. Withinness
#322-1: 1960 Chicago Open Class 2:1
#322-2: 1960 Chicago Open Class 2:2

## 6. Bringing Grace into Active Expression
#246-2: 1959 Maui Advanced Work 4:2

## 7. The Power to Become the Son of God
#140-1: 1956 First Steinway Hall Practitioner Class 1:1
#140-2: 1956 First Steinway Hall Practitioner Class 1:2

## 8. Rising Above "This World"
#142-2: 1956 First Steinway Hall Practitioner Class 3:2

## 9. Spiritual Dominion
#272-2: 1959 Vancouver Open Class 1:2

## 10. The Meaning of Prayer
#284-1: 1959 Lausanne Closed Class 2:1

## 11. Breaking the Bonds of Humanhood
#375-2: 1960 Melbourne Closed Class 1:2

## 12. The Prince of Peace
#443-1: 1961 Hawaiian Village Open Class 7:1

Made in the USA
Monee, IL
13 August 2020